International Intracorporate Pricing

Jeffrey S. Arpan

The Praeger Special Studies program—utilizing the most modern and efficient book production techniques and a selective worldwide distribution network—makes available to the academic, government, and business communities significant, timely research in U.S. and international economic, social, and political development.

International Intracorporate Pricing
Non-American Systems and Views

Praeger Publishers   New York   Washington   London

PRAEGER PUBLISHERS
111 Fourth Avenue, New York, N.Y. 10003, U.S.A.
5, Cromwell Place, London S.W.7, England

Published in the United States of America in 1972
by Praeger Publishers, Inc.

Library of Congress Catalog Card Number: 72-79558

Printed in the United States of America

The author takes this opportunity to express his appreciation to the many people who assisted him in conducting this study.

International intracorporate pricing spans many disciplines. The broad scope of this subject required the assistance of people with knowledge of equal breadth, and this researcher was indeed fortunate to find three principal advisers with such credentials. Lyle Dieterle, professor of accounting at Indiana University, was particularly helpful in the area of international accounting and in arranging interviews with partners of the eight international accounting firms. Richard Farmer, chairman of the International Business Department, supplied encouragement and a wealth of helpful ideas from beginning to end. Special recognition is due Professor L. Leslie Waters, who served most ably and courageously as the major adviser for this study. His personal guidance, counseling, and friendship were invaluable in initiating and completing this research and throughout the author's course of study at Indiana University. No words of gratitude will ever be able to acknowledge his role as adviser and friend.

Many others at Indiana University deserve recognition. Professors Lee Nehrt and Sam Frumer sparked my initial interest in international transfer pricing, while Professors Robert Stevens, Zuhayr Mikdashi, and Mr. W. D. Hogue offered many helpful suggestions and comments during the course of the research. Many personal colleagues, no longer at Indiana, were also extremely helpful. David Ricks (Ohio State University), Joe Vogel (Ford Motor Company), and Donald Patton (University of Montreal) deserve particular recognition.

My gratitude also extends to the many corporate executives who participated in this study but who, by necessity, must remain anonymous. Participants who can be mentioned are members of the "big eight" accounting firms: George Thieman of Arthur Anderson & Co.; Donald Goss of Arthur Young & Co.; Ed Ryan of Ernst and Ernst; Costas Nicolaides of Haskins and Sells; Julian Phelps and Herbert Rosenberg of Lybrand, Ross Bros. and Montgomery; David Thompson of Peat, Marwick, Mitchell and Co.; Ted Wilkinson of Price Waterhouse and Company; and James Johnston and Earl Pontius of Touche Ross and Co. William Person of Business International Corporation was also a particularly helpful contributor.

Funds for field research were supplied by a generous grant from the International Business Research Institute of Indiana University, Professor Schuyler Otteson, director. The author is greatly indebted to the Institute's executive committee for this grant and the expression of confidence it implied.

Finally, my utmost appreciation goes to my daughter, Laurie, whose tender age will perhaps spare her unpleasant memories of a too-often absent father, and to my parents, whose unwavering support and faith in me has finally begun to bear fruit. It is to them that this study is dedicated.

CONTENTS

LIST OF TABLES

LIST OF CHARTS

International
Intracorporate Pricing

THE PROBLEM

The yearly operations of a multinational firm require a considerable amount of trade between the parent and its subsidiaries. The parent sells and buys a variety of goods and services to and from its subsidiaries, the prices of which might appear irrelevant at first glance. As long as the performance of the entire organization is being evaluated, it does not appear important to determine which part of the organization contributes how much of the total profit. However, from the perspective of national tax authorities, it does make a difference where the income eventually ends up within a corporation. Careful price manipulation of intra-company transfers enables corporations to report either profits or losses for their operations in a given country at a given point in time, often resulting in substantial income tax savings.

As this researcher learned more about intra-corporation pricing, several other variables emerged as important factors. Customs duties, exchange restrictions, competitive advantages, and threats of expropriation, devaluation, and revaluation were

several major non-tax considerations cited by
U.S. multinational firms.[1] In any event cost and
price details must be known for optimal resource
allocation. Determining prices for intracorporate
transfers is a highly sensitive and increasingly
important decision-making function for the firm,
and it has many implications and ramifications for
both external and internal parties.

The small amount of research that has already
been done in this area has only focused on U.S.
multinational firms. Although these firms conduct
a substantial amount of the world's international
business, it represents only a portion of the total. At present the U.S. share is decreasing and
in many areas it has already been surpassed by non-
U.S. multinational firms.[2] Because a considerable
amount of international business is conducted by
these latter firms, they are the subject of this
study. The specific purpose of this study is to
investigate the intracorporate pricing systems of
non-U.S. multinational companies in order to obtain
a better understanding of the total problem.

BACKGROUND OF THE PROBLEM

One of the noticeable and economically significant developments of the twentieth century has been
the phenomenal growth of corporations, not only in
quantity and quality but also in sheer physical
size. Mergers, acquisitions, consolidations, and
nearly exponential growths of individual corporations have created problems for both antitrust and
Internal Revenue Service officials as well as corporate executives.

A shift has been made to more decentralized
operations and management in order to lighten the
increasing load on top management. A profit-center
system has also been established to measure, evaluate, and motivate these divisional managements.
Subsequently the need has arisen for a rational system to arrive at "an optimal price" for intracompany

transfers of goods and services at varying stages
of production and distribution.

A basic problem occurs whenever there is more
than one profit center. Transfers between profit
centers approach a zero sum game situation in the
sense that any increase in one division's profits
must come at the expense of another's. This type
of internal competition can easily lead to internal
fighting, power struggles, failures to undertake
profitable opportunities, and a general increase in
management headaches.

Top management's objective has been to devise
methods that would satisfy the goal of divisional
managers to earn adequate profits for their divisions while also furthering the corporate goals.[3]
Some systems have functioned well domestically and
have provided a logical foundation for good control
systems. However, in multinational operations it
is more difficult to apply the profit-center system
for control and evaluation purposes. When a firm
operates across national boundaries and in differing economic, social, and political environments,
new and further complicating dimensions are added
to its already complex domestic set. Opportunities
for profit maximization can arise that may override
the significance of the existing control system, or
the foreign environment may contain threats to the
operation, thereby necessitating a different ration-
ale for making management decisions. The basic
transfer pricing problem is the same whether a firm
operates domestically or internationally. What differs is the number of variables and constraints
that should be considered in the price-determination
process.

Taking the above into consideration, one might
expect that all multinational firms faced the same
problems and would, therefore, have similar intracorporate pricing systems. But this is not the
case. The most obvious reason is that the intracorporate pricing decision is only one of many decisions that involve the maneuvering of liquid

assets within a corporation and only one of an even
larger number of decisions dealing with the basic
functional operations of a firm. Each individual
corporation has a mixture of goals and constraints
that are unique and that necessitate different
strategies and outlooks.

Transfer prices affect the net profitability
of the firm so significantly that these decisions
are made high in the corporate hierarchy, irrespec-
tive of its parent's nationality. Although the
title of this decision-maker may vary--from President to Financial Vice-President to Comptroller to
Treasurer--the person who has the responsibility
for overall financial management of the company
also has the responsibility for setting intracorporate prices.

The continuing importance of the problem can
be attributed to several developments. First, the
increased awareness of the manipulative possibilities of transfer pricing by numerous outside groups
has led management to show greater interest in and
surveillance of company practices, especially in
areas where national governments have an interest:
income tax, tariffs, antitrust, and political opinion. Because income tax officials want to receive
"their fair share" of tax revenues from a company,
they are not favorably disposed to the idea of a
firm's profits being understated in a given country
because of artificially inflated intracorporate
prices (which overstate the costs of the buying
firm and hence understate its net income). Customs
officials, on the other hand, do not want to lose
revenue from the duties assessed on the value of
transferred goods if the intracorporate prices are
artificially deflated. Antitrust officials are
concerned about potential dumping violations and
price discrimination practices made possible by
managed intracorporate prices. Finally, other government officials may become interested when their
constituents and financial backers have vested interests that are being adversely affected.

Other significant non-governmental groups affected by transfer pricing are creditors, labor unions, and investors. The creditors and investors must determine how much of a firm's profit may have resulted from deflated intracorporate prices. Labor unions, on the other hand, want to know whether the profits are understated because of the use of artificially inflated intracorporate prices. In sum, many groups are affected by intracorporate pricing systems, but few have direct access to information about them. Although this study will not help those who want to find out about the intracorporate pricing system of a particular firm, it should help them to learn about the various systems in use, their different effects, and their general trends.

DEFINITIONS

Before proceeding further, it might be well to define and clarify a few things. There has been discussion among academicians in the field of international business about the need to distinguish a multinational firm from an international firm and about differentiating these two entities from one simply engaged in some degree of international business.[4] Because the term "multinational firm" is used throughout this study, it is essential to clarify its meaning.

N. K. Bruck and F. A. Lees differentiate on the basis of international sales.[5] Those corporations having more than 50 percent of their sales abroad are classified as international, those with 25 to 50 percent as multinational, and those with 10 to 25 percent as having significant operations.

Slightly more pejorative connotations have been given in the Task Force report <u>Foreign Ownership and the Structure of Canadian Industry</u>.

There is the global corporation,
with such pervasive operations that

it is beyond the effective reach of
national policies of any country, free
to some extent to make decisions in
the interest of corporate efficiency
alone. . . . The multinational corporation is, in a genuine sense, sensitive to local traditions and re-
specting local jurisdictions and policies. . . . The national corporation
insists on the primacy of the methods
it uses at home, and even the laws of
the home country.[6]

Charles P. Kindleberger defines the three in a
less pejorative way and perhaps most clearly for
general use.

The international corporation has no
country to which it owes more loyalty
than any other, nor any country where
it feels completely at home. It
equalizes the return on its invested
capital in every country, after adjustment for risk which is free of
the myopia that says home investment
is automatically risk free and all
foreign investments are risky. It is
willing to speculate against the currency of the head office because it
regards holdings of cash anywhere as
subject to exchange risks which
should be hedged.
The multinational firm seeks to
be a good citizen of each country
where it has operations . . . hires
local executives to more than a token
extent, possibly admits local capital.
When efficiency and citizenship occasionally diverge, the requirements of
citizenship are to take precedence.
The national firm with foreign
operations knows where it belongs.
First and foremost it is a citizen
of a particular country. Foreign

> operations are small in the total
> scheme of things. . . . It may have
> substantial foreign ownership inter-
> ests, but it feels at home only in
> one country, and substantially alien
> everywhere else.[7]

Most of the firms included in this study best
fit Kindleberger's definition of a multinational
corporation, but many are more national than multinational. Thus the term "multinational" as used
here does not correspond precisely to any of the
foregoing definitions. Instead, multinational is
defined as a corporation with a manufacturing subsidiary in at least one country other than the site
of the home office. With this definition, multinational could include all the firms in both Kindleberger's and the Task Force's continua, but perhaps
not all of those in Lees and Bruck's. The critical
distinction is in the manufacturing characteristic
and not in the percentage of sales or type of attitude. The major reason for this distinction is
that only firms with manufacturing subsidiaries
were included in this study; therefore, generalizations about multinational companies drawn from it
could possibly be misconstrued or misinterpreted.

The term "non-U.S. multinational company" then
refers to a multinational company whose home office
is not located within the continental boundaries of
the United States. The home office, also called
the "parent," is the headquarters for the entire
operation and the center of the decision-making
process. Although some companies claim to be equally at home in many countries, they have only one
home office, and almost without exception it is the
home office that makes the final decision about intracorporate pricing.

Intracorporate pricing refers to the value-
determination process for transfers made within a
corporate family, as between the parent and subsidiary or among subsidiaries. It encompasses the
transfer of loans and advances, services, and the

use and sale of tangible and intangible property. The term is also used synonymously with "transfer pricing."*

TENTATIVE HYPOTHESES

The goal of this study was to investigate the non-U.S. systems of international intracorporate pricing. Consequently, the number of hypotheses to be tested was limited. It was anticipated that the findings would generate hypotheses that could be tested in future research. Therefore, major emphasis was given to the following hypotheses.

1. All multinational companies face the same environmental problems with respect to international transfer pricing.

2. Not all multinational corporations perceive the importance of problems in the same way.

3. Differences in perceived importance are a function of different cultural influences.

4. Cultural differences lead to different international intracorporate pricing systems.

5. No single transfer pricing system is optimal for all multinational corporations.

LIMITATIONS AND DELIMITATIONS

Intracorporate pricing is only one of several ways to maneuver liquid assets around the various

---

*Most writers define transfer pricing to include both intracorporate and intercorporate sales, while others differentiate on some basis, usually percentage ownership of the subsidiary. The distinction is largely academic and will not be discussed here. To avoid confusion, however, "transfer pricing" has the larger connotation in this study.

parts of a corporation. Dividend remittances, for
example, constitute a major alternative method and
one that is frequently used. By limiting this
study to transfer pricing, some parts of the total
decision-making arena are necessarily excluded.
However, transfer pricing broadly defined includes
not only the vast majority of alternatives but also
the most frequent ones and, to a significant degree,
those that determine how much of a dividend can be
declared (or even if one needs to be declared at
all). Corroborating the significance of transfer
pricing as a focus, David Zenoff and Jack Zwick
comment:

> Although current data are unavailable,
> in 1963 U.S. companies sold approxi-
> mately $5 billion worth of finished
> and unfinished goods, components and
> supplies to their affiliates in for-
> eign countries, and probably many hun-
> dreds of millions of dollars' worth
> in addition were sold by affiliates
> of the companies to their sister firms
> in their countries. Intracompany
> sales are the single most important
> method of effecting a movement of
> capital between countries in which
> companies have operations.[8]

A second limitation emerges from corporate management's sensitivity to this topic. Whereas dividends are essentially public information, intracorporate prices are not: they constitute one of the
most secretive operations of the firm. This research, therefore, was limited to those firms that
were willing to participate and had to be conducted
largely on their terms. This undoubtedly contribu-
ted a bias to the information received and made it
difficult to compare responses. (These difficulties will be discussed in Chapters 3 and 5.) The
method selected was the best available considering
the fact that the companies' participation was en-
tirely voluntary and that the topic is secretive.
A check on the reliability of the information received and an additional view of the general problem

was obtained from the eight major international accounting firms. Their knowledge and assistance
greatly increased the reliability and scope of the
study.

A third limitation stems from the nature and
location of the corporate operations. Only non-
U.S. multinational firms are included in this study,
thereby excluding (1) firms with only sales offices or other forms of distributorship in the United
States, (2) firms with manufacturing subsidiaries
and business operations in other countries but not
in the United States, and (3) all U.S. multinational
corporations. The latter firms are excluded because
they have already been studied in various degrees
by other researchers (see Chapter 2) and additional
study of their systems would not contribute substantially to existing knowledge. The exclusion of
firms with only nonmanufacturing operations is not
really a restriction on information but only on
numbers. That is, a typical manufacturing subsidiary may simultaneously buy and sell raw materials,
semifinished components, and final goods from its
parent, receive or make loans and advances to its
parent, and even buy and sell management advice.
In short, its operations and attendant problems en-
compass those of the sales office as well as other
problems. Therefore, more information can be obtained at lower cost by dealing with the manufacturing subsidiaries.

There are two reasons for limiting firms to
those having U.S. manufacturing subsidiaries.
First, it provides an opportunity to compare how
foreign companies with U.S. subsidiaries view the
transfer pricing problem in relation to U.S. companies with foreign subsidiaries (and information
on the latter is already available). Secondly,
correspondence and follow-up interviews are facili-
tated by the firms' geographical proximity and
their managements' command of the English language.

Last, there were financial and time limitations. It might have been preferable in some ways

for the research to have been conducted at the corporate headquarters, rather than by correspondence
and interviews with their U.S. subsidiaries. But
to do this would have been beyond the financial resources of this researcher. In several instances,
the U.S. subsidiaries were larger than their non-
U.S. parents. In most cases, little information
was probably lost by interviewing the U.S. subsidiaries. The high concentration of subsidiaries with
different parent nationalities in the New York area
enabled the researcher to save substantial time and
money.

To summarize, the scope of any research requires realistic focusing. Many firms maneuver
their liquid assets within, and there are many alternative ways to accomplish shifts that, by design,
have been left out of this study. To investigate
individually all of these firms and all of these alternatives clearly would have required more money,
time, and access than was available. By focusing
on the non-U.S. systems of international intracorporate pricing, an important part of the total picture is added.

AN OVERVIEW OF THE STUDY

Transfer pricing is rooted in accounting theory but touches many other disciplines as well.
Anything from in-depth treatment to passing refer-
ences can be found in most textbooks on the principles of finance, accounting, marketing, or management. Secondary and tertiary treatments, including
the international dimension, can be found in professional business literature.

The initial research for this study necessi-
tated consulting the literature in many disciplines.
The scattered nature of the information on transfer
pricing makes it difficult for the search to be in-
clusive in all respects. In spite of this drawback,
which is certainly not unique to the problem of
transfer pricing, the main currents and developments

in this field have been identified. The published information is placed in historical perspective and grouped into works dealing with domestic and international systems. Each area is then divided into theory and field research. The review of the literature in Chapter 2 provides information on all related aspects for both the remotely curious and the highly interested.

Information gaps remain in several areas; the largest is the role, systems, and ramifications in intracorporate pricing in international business. Within this area, there is an even greater lack of information on non-U.S. intracorporate pricing systems, the topic of this study. Consequently, field research was mandatory. First, firms were asked to identify the major variables they consider in formulating their transfer prices and to rank them in order of importance. These replies constituted the basis for making industry and national comparisons, which were then submitted to the eight major international accounting firms for comment. The researcher than incorporated the field data and comments with his own analysis to form the conclusions of the study.

The details of the entire research method are described and analyzed in Chapter 3. The method employed may leave something to be desired from a statistical point of view, but the nature of the problem and the size of the information gap interacted in such a way as to determine the specific research method. Information about the characteristics of the population and sample used in this study is also included in Chapter 3. The individual firms by necessity had to remain anonymous, thereby precluding the use of certain types of descriptive analysis.

The results obtained by applying the research techniques to the specific problem are described and discussed in Chapter 4. This chapter includes comments made by the individual firms about their own systems and their impressions of the general

problems and trends influencing other companies, as
well as observations made by the international accounting firms, which largely substantiated the
statements of the individual companies. Some related findings and comments on the parent-subsidiary
relationships of these multinational firms are also
included, which should interest anyone studying the
multinational corporation or comparative business
operations.

Finally, Chapter 5 synthesizes the entire study
and comments on its successes, failures, significance, and applicability. It closes by identifying
some unanswered questions to be taken up by future
researchers.

NOTES

1.   See James Shulman, "Transfer Pricing in
Multinational Business" (unpublished Ph.D. dissertation, Harvard University, 1966); and Solving International Pricing Problems (New York: Business International Corporation, 1965).

2.   In particular, see Stanley E. Rolf and
Walter Damm, The Multinational Corporation in the
World Economy (New York: Praeger Publishers, 1970),
pp. 9-10; and Rainer Hellmann, The Challenge to
U.S. Dominance of the International Corporation
(Cambridge, Mass.:   Dunellen, 1970), Chapters 1
and 2.

3.   See Shulman, "Transfer Pricing in International Business," Chapter 1.

4.   For excellent summaries of various definitions, see Hellmann, The Challenge to U.S. Dominance
of the International Corporation, pp. 22-27; and
Rolfe and Damm, The Multinational Corporation in
the World Economy, pp. 16-17.

5.   N. K. Bruck and F. A. Lees, "Foreign Con-
tent of U.S. Corporate Activities," Financial Ana-
lysts Journal (September-October 1966).

6. <u>Foreign Ownership and the Structure of the Canadian Industry</u>, Report of the Task Force on the Canadian Industry (Ottawa: Queen's Printer, 1968), p. 3.

7. Charles P. Kindleberger, <u>American Business Abroad</u> (New Haven: Yale University Press, 1969), pp. 180-82.

8. David Zenoff and Jack Zwick, <u>International Financial Management</u> (Englewood Cliffs, N.J.: Prentice-Hall, 1969), p. 428.

INTRODUCTION

No specific studies could be found on the intracorporate pricing systems of non-U.S. multinational firms, although there is much related literature.   Academically, transfer pricing is a cost accounting concept and receives varying degrees of
treatment in cost and managerial accounting texts.[1]
These books do not include the international dimension of the problem but do provide basic information on domestic systems.

Two of the better theoretical and applied
treatments are not found in accounting texts.   An
excellent theoretical discussion, both verbal and
graphical, is presented by David Solomons in his
book Divisional Performance, Management and Control.[2]   Some of the best applied analysis appears
in the text Management Control Systems by Anthony,
Dearden, and Vancil.[3]   The thoroughness of both
treatments is not surprising, for transfer pricing
received more attention outside the field of cost
accounting, at least in its early stages of development.

The international dimension has not been discussed extensively, either theoretically or empiri-
cally. Graduate-level texts in the field of international business now include some discussion of
the problem, but they do not propose any solutions
nor attempt to modify the existing body of domestic
theory.[4]

Transfer pricing is also discussed in a myriad
of professional business journals and accounting
bulletins. Each deals with a specific aspect of
the problem, such as tax considerations, antitrust
implications, or the effects on management performance. None of them discuss the non-U.S. systems
of international intracorporate pricing, however.

This chapter will trace the historical development of the written works on transfer pricing and
then categorize and discuss them in greater detail
on the basis of their orientation--domestic or international.

THE HISTORICAL DEVELOPMENT

Major works on intracorporate pricing only began to appear after 1954, although the problem had
been discussed as early as 1929.[5] The major question raised at that time was whether costs or market
prices should be used for pricing the goods transferred among departments. It is interesting to
note that this central question has still not been
answered after four decades of research.

Between 1930 and 1955, one major article was
published on transfer pricing. H. N. Broom proposed a method for eliminating intracompany profits
resulting from inventory transfers,[6] but his article
was limited to describing his method and giving examples of its application.

Definitive works on intracorporate pricing began to appear in the mid-1950s; the first ones
dealt with decentralization and transfer pricing.

In two remarkably similar but separate articles, Paul Cook and Joel Dean each highlighted the problems that arise when transfers occur within a decentralized firm.[7] Each author presented a concise description and analysis of the major types of systems: those using market-based prices, those using cost-based prices, and those using some combination of the two. They also came to essentially the same conclusion: that to minimize the problems caused by intercompany pricing in a decentralized firm, decentralization should take place on a divisional basis, with each division operating as a profit center and using competitive market-based prices for intracompany transfers.

It was Jack Hirschleifer, however, who first theorized about the transfer pricing problem. In two articles, he set out rigorous economic treatments of the intracorporate pricing problems in differing market situations.[8] Hirshleifer's major conclusion was that the market-price approach recommended by Cook and Dean could correctly be used only where the commodity being transferred was produced in a purely competitive market. If the market was imperfectly competitive or did not exist for the transferred good, then the correct procedure was to transfer the goods either at marginal cost or at some price between it and the market price. Disagreeing with Cook and Dean in another respect, Hirschleifer stated that the rule of pricing at market was the one most frequently adopted by business.

An article by Harold Bierman and a second one by Paul Cook brought to a close the 1950s' treatment of intracorporate pricing.[9] Cook defended his earlier recommendation of market-based prices, while Bierman walked a tightrope beautifully by stating that any alternative was reasonable so long as the selection was made after the firm had determined the purpose for using the information.

Five of these six pioneering articles appeared in nonaccounting journals. This pattern has not changed substantially over the years, indicating

the cross-disciplinary nature of the transfer pricing problem. It also suggests that those who are
responsible for making the pricing decisions are
high-level officers rather than cost accountants.

The major onslaught of articles began in 1960.
Forty-four appeared in various professional journals
in the subsequent ten-year period. Up to 1966 the
majority dealt with the effects of intracorporate
pricing on divisional performance, evaluation, and
profit measurement.[10] This period also marked the
entance of the National Association of Accountants'
Bulletin on the subject.[11]

There were several notable exceptions: Nicholas
Dopuch and David Drake introduced the first mathematical approach for solving the transfer pricing
problem;[12] J. R. Gould extended Hirschleifer's economic analysis to include the case where there were
costs of using an outside market;[13] and Willard
Stone introduced some of the legal implications of
transfer pricing.[14]

During the early 1960s the discussion of transfer pricing also began to appear in business textbooks. The earliest in-depth treatment was done by
Charles Horngren in 1962,[15] although the subject
had been included in other accounting texts as early as 1954.[16]

Of particular relevance to this research was
the appearance of the first works on international
intracorporate pricing. The pioneering efforts
were James Shulman's doctoral dissertation[17] and a
study conducted by Business International Corporation,[18] both in the mid-1960s. Shulman discussed
the problems peculiar to international business
that complicate the transfer pricing decision and
reached the conclusion that no single system can be
optimal for all firms. He did not propose any solution or new theory. The Business International
study was more thorough, included a much larger number of firms, but reached essentially the same conclusion as Shulman. Neither study included non-U.S.

multinational companies, but they did lay the foundation for further research by identifying the major problem areas for transfer pricing that had not been explored.

The major emphasis after 1965 was on taxes and, more specifically, the effect of changes in the U.S. Treasury regulations on intracompany pricing.[19] The best single source of articles is the February 1968 issue of the <u>Journal of Taxation</u>.[20] Other articles deal specifically with the Eli Lilly case, which was the first major court victory for the government in intracorporate pricing disputes.[21]

The non-tax oriented articles on intracorporate pricing ranged in scope from general explanations to rigorous, highly theoretical, economic extensions.[22] Those with an international orientation included James Shulman's "When the Price Is Wrong by Design,"[23] James Greene's "Intercorporate Pricing across National Frontiers,"[24] and H. M. Schoenfeld's "Some Special Accounting Problems of Multinational Enterprises."[25] None of these articles discussed non-U.S. firms, and none came up with any viable solution. This is essentially the situation at present.

DOMESTIC SYSTEMS

Theoretical Works

The underlying theory for domestic transfer pricing systems was best explained by Jack Hirschleifer, who arrived at definitive solutions for determining optimal transfer prices in four different market situations by using economic analysis and concluded:

1. If there is a single joint level of output to be determined, output should be such that the sum of divisional marginal costs equals the marginal revenue in the final market. Thus transfer prices must equal the marginal cost of the selling division.

2. If there is technological and demand independence and if there is a perfectly competitive market, the transfer price should equal the market price.

3. Where there exists technological dependence, there can be no solution.

4. Where there exists demand dependence, the solution lies between marginal cost and market price.[26]

In a later article Hirschleifer derived the solution to the case where the demands are related (number 4 above) by introducing a series of bounties and taxes on the departments.

It is important to note that Hirschleifer's optimal rules for transfer prices lead to correct output adjustments only at the margin, even under ideal conditions. Also, his analysis applies only to domestic systems and is not appropriate for decisions regarding international transfers.

Andrew Philippakas and Howard Thompson added to the theoretical discussion of the use of internal rewards 14 years later.[27] They developed special reward functions and a resultant system of transfer prices, leading to overall profit (or revenue) maximization subject to a profit constraint. Their system works by rewarding departments on the basis of their output, subject to a departmental profit constraint, such that the sum of the required department profits equals the total required profit by the firm.

Three points are worth noting. First, their model applies only to a single buying and selling department, a number of producing departments supplying one selling department, and a series of producing departments each of which adds to and passes on a product toward a final selling department. Second, Philippakas and Thompson assume that in all cases production sells only internally and that the

flow of product continues in only one direction.
There are many exceptions to these restrictions,
and so the value of the analysis is diminished accordingly. Third, the model is not applicable to
the international environment, which they acknowledge.

The analysis presented by David Solomons
brought together most of the work done by Hirschleifer.[28] Nothing more advanced was added, but he
did discuss a few additional elementary cases.

J. R. Gould's article dealt with the situation
where there are costs of using an outside market.[29]
He agreed with the earlier writers that where there
are perfectly competitive outside markets, trans-
ferring at market prices is the well-established
and optimal rule, so long as the divisions are free
to sell inside and outside the firm. He wanted to
solve the problem that arises when the net prices
obtainable outside the firm differ for the buying
and selling divisions. Gould acknowledged that he
was unable to devise a system that did not significantly reduce the delegation, supposedly fostered
by transfer pricing, thereby making the institution
of intracorporate pricing seem hardly worthwhile.
He further stated that transfer pricing was an in-
appropriate method of decentralization if it was believed that divisional profits were an effective
stimulus, that no great economies could be made in
information transmission and processing, and that
serious losses arose from nonoptimal levels of output. Gould's analysis, although thorough, is applicable in only two situations: that of the perfectly competitive outside market and that of centralized decision-making. It does not work in the
case of international business.

Dopuch and Drake went a step beyond the econo-
mists by discussing the application of a mathematical approach to intracorporate pricing. They dealt
with the use of shadow prices and the decomposition
principle in both linear and nonlinear programming
applications.[30] They concluded that shadow prices

did not lead to optimal output decisions and that
the decomposition principle did not work in practice because it was too time-consuming. Dopuch and
Drake made no attempt to develop a better mathematical technique to implement an optimal system of
transfer pricing; their purpose was only to consoli-
date the material on transfer pricing in order to
evaluate how linear and nonlinear programming techniques could be applied.[31]

Problems with Decentralization and Profit Centers

Decentralization based on departmental or divisional profit maximization has inherent motivational
inadequacies in terms of the firm's overall optimality. When separate parts of a corporation are being
judged on profit and also participate in determining
transfer prices, there is the incentive to violate
overall optimality for the sake of individual bene-
fit.* This point is well illustrated in the writings of Joel Dean, J. R. Gould, Andrew Philippakas
and Howard Thompson, Paul Cook, John Dearden, and
Jean P. Boyer. They agree that intracompany pricing
and accountability should be geared to maximizing
the cooperative effort of the entire organization,
but they disagree on which type of system is best.

Joel Dean opts for negotiated arm's-length
prices after reviewing the advantages and disadvantages of all other types.[32] John Dearden prefers
the use of incremental costs because arm's-length
prices tend to be irrelevant and lead to goal in-
congruence.[33] His marginal approach considers how
much the total cost will increase if the contem-
plated activity is added, or how much the total
cost will decrease if the activity is discontinued.

----

*Hirschleifer and Cook have both discussed in-
stances in which the rational action of divisional
managers was not consistent with company profit
maximization even though it was consistent with
divisional profit maximization.

Paul Cook and Joseph Wodjak both feel that the use
of market prices is optimal, because it best meets
the needs of the total organization and is acceptable to tax authorities.[34] Frederick Finney comes
full circle in recommending actual manufacturing
cost, although he admits that it does not provide a
good measure of operating efficiency.[35]

Several writers have divided opinions. Hirschleifer qualifies his recommendation of market prices
by stating that under less than perfectly competitive
conditions, the marginal cost is best.[36] James
Fremgen feels that the appropriate transfer price
depends on the purpose for which the price is sought:
The full production cost should be used when the ob-
ject is to produce financial statements that conform
with generally accepted accounting principles; the
market price should be used when the goal is to evaluate individual divisions as unique, operating entities; and the avoidable cost should be used when the
objective is to provide a basis for company-wide
decision-making.[37] Harold Bierman reaches a similar
conclusion that all system orientations are reasonable and that a choice should be made only after the
proposed use of the information has been determined.[38]
His recommendations coincide with Fremgen's except
that he prefers marginal cost to avoidable cost for
general decision-making.

The characteristics, advantages, and disadvantages of all these orientations have been discussed
at length by these writers. Nothing has been resolved; nothing material has been added. The prospects for either are dim. All that can be said is
that two conditions must prevail in order to prevent
profit centers from increasing their profits at the
expense of the company's overall position. First,
transfers must be made if they increase the profit
of the company, and second, these transfers must not
be forced on profit centers if they decrease the
profit of the company.[39]

Neither the theory nor its application seems to
be able to prove which type of system orientation is

best for all firms. An outside force (such as the
Internal Revenue Service) may be required to settle
the issue.

Taxation

By the inclusion or omission of an element of
profit in a transfer price, the net income can be
retained in one corporation or shifted from subsidiary to parent, from parent to subsidiary, or from
one subsidiary to another. The decision to use one
type of system affects the amount of net income and
consequently the amount of tax paid by a "family"
of corporations. This manipulation of income continues to trigger the interest and attention of the
Internal Revenue Service.

Section 482 of the 1954 U.S. Internal Revenue
Service Code deals specifically with intracompany
pricing. There were two basic reasons for its adoption: (1) to prevent tax evasion by firms that
split their income so that no division has an income of more than $25,000 or that operate in a coun-
try whose tax rate is less than that of the United
States, and (2) to ensure that the U.S. government
will receive its fair share of taxes on income
earned by a multinational company. Many experts
felt that the precedent-setting requirement that
transfer pricing be the equivalent of the fair market value for tax purposes would restrict intracorporate pricing to this one method. The only con-
tingencies were whether the director of the Internal
Revenue Service would strictly apply the rule and
whether his rulings would be upheld by the courts.[40]
The writings of Warren Keegen, D. E. Cook, Robert
Holtzman, Harry Mansfield, Stanley Surrey, and the
tax commissioner, Sheldon Cohen, were all explana-
tory. They described the four methods for determining the market price that are acceptable to the IRS
and explained the tests of "reasonableness" for cal-
culating taxable income.

Other writers began to point out that the
specification of market prices was not as inflexible

or critical as it had originally appeared. It soon
became evident that the reasonableness of the division of net income within a corporate family was
the most important factor considered by the IRS and
not any particular method of transfer pricing.
This major point was made by Walter O'Connor, Warren
Keegen, and Paul Seghers (in his 1967 article), particularly in reference to the Eli Lilly decision.
The specific ruling of the court was that Eli Lilly
was guilty under the second purpose of Section 482--
not clearly reflecting its net income, rather than
evading taxes.[41]

The Lilly case emphasized that even sound business reasons for adopting a price on intracorporate
transfers would not insulate a firm from the reallo-
cation of Section 482. The court also set the criteria for determining how the IRS should consider
income by indicating that any measure such as "fair
and reasonable" or "fairly arrived at" must be defined within the framework of "fair and reasonable
as among unrelated parties."

The IRS and the court both failed to decide
the issue on the type of transfer price to be used.
If other than market prices are used, the burden of
proof falls on the taxpayer. If the resultant division of income is reasonable, however, it appears
that firms will not have to fear intervention from
the U.S. Internal Revenue Service.

The Use of Multiple
Systems and Prices

No single transfer pricing orientation works
equally well for all firms, or even for an individual firm, at all times. If circumstances change,
it may be desirable (profitable) for a firm to
change its system. Even if conditions do not
change, no single transfer pricing system can satisfy all internal and external purposes. No one
has actually recommended adoption of a multiple
system, although some have discussed it.

The major drawbacks to a multiple system are
that it creates a mountain of book work, confusion,
and antitrust problems.[42] If a firm wants to use
marginal cost for decision-making purposes, market
prices for profit center evaluation or tax purposes,
and full cost for consolidated financial statements,
it would have to keep separate accounts for intracompany transfers, intracompany payables and receiv-
ables, and intracompany inventories on hand at both
cost and transfer price value. The resultant confusion on the divisional level would be considerable.

The firm also runs the risk of antitrust viola-
tion if it maintains one orientation but varies the
price to different buyers. U.S. antitrust law extends to intracompany pricing in cases where the
parent sells to its subsidiaries at lower prices
than it would sell to nonrelated companies (provided
that the subsidiaries do not perform services that
would not be performed by the nonrelated firms).[43]

Summary

The domestic theory does not provide a clear
answer to the transfer pricing problem. No single
system emerges as appropriate for all cases and multiple systems do not appear feasible. If it does
not work well in theory, how well can it work in
practice? To answer this question, let us turn to
actual studies of systems in use.

Domestic Studies

The most comprehensive study of domestic systems was conducted by the National Industrial Conference Board.[44] One-half of the firms interviewed
used cost in some form as the basis for their intracorporate prices, one-third used market prices, and
the remainder used some combination of the two.
Transfers were made at cost when the selling division was a cost center, but with some profit allowance if the selling division was a profit center.

The advantages cited by those who used the cost
basis were that the system was simple to administer

and understand, the data were more readily available, and it met the requirement of government contracts and regulatory agencies. The disadvantages were that the system tended to weaken managerial authority, reduced the incentive for cost reduction, interfered with the evaluation of divisional performance, and induced opposition by divisional managers.

Those employing market prices for intracompany transfers said that the advantages of their orientation were that it was consistent with decentralized profit responsibility, permitted a valid appraisal of divisional performance, identified unprofitable or inefficient operations, and provided greater incentive for cost reduction. The disadvantages were that it was often difficult to determine a market price, product cost information was lost as goods flowed from one division to another, and inadequate margins of profit often occurred at the last division in competitive markets. Most companies in the study allowed outside purchases but only within limits. Permission was usually granted in cases where the internal supply was inadequate and where there were better outside prices.

A very extensive study of internal transfer pricing was done by Willard Stone in 1957.[45] His sample of 350 companies was taken from the Federal Trade Commission's list of the 1,000 largest manufacturing companies. Stone concentrated on those corporations with assets exceeding $50 million. He found both market- and cost-based prices used widely while negotiated prices were used infrequently and only in supplemental ways. He also found that the majority of companies had more than one pricing method.

Stone concluded that the income tax regulations should not seriously restrict the use of a transfer pricing method chosen for business purposes and that, in the absence of restraint of trade, antitrust laws should have little influence upon the selection. He pointed out that foreign customs

laws require the use of specific pricing methods
where applicable, however.

Other writers have discussed the systems in
use, although most of them have not offered statistical support. Warren Keegen reported that the
"cost-plus" method was the one most frequently
used,[46] while Paul Cook said that direct cost and
market prices were the most popular.[47] Neither
author supplied information about the size or characteristics of his sample or offered substantiation
for his statements. The studies by the National
Industrial Conference Board and Willard Stone thus
remain the most comprehensive and reliable sources
on in-use domestic transfer pricing systems.

INTERNATIONAL SYSTEMS

Theoretical Works

There is no theory of international intracorporate pricing. No one has attempted to extend the
body of domestic theory to include the international
dimension. No one has developed a complete theory
solely for international transfer pricing.

The only theoretical work in this field has
been done by David Rutenberg.[48] His research dealt
with the optimal use of tax havens, bilateral tax
treaties, nonuniform treatment of income received
from abroad, and national differences in income tax
rates, import duties, and border taxes. In his
model, liquid assets are maneuvered among subsidiaries to minimize the taxes paid to the world minus
the interest received. The movement is accomplished
by manipulating transfer prices, managerial fees and
royalties, dividends, and intersubsidiary loans.*

----

*Rutenberg restricts "transfer pricing" to the
pricing of goods, which is a narrower definition
than the one used in this study. His decision-
making framework is similar though, because he

Recognizing that intervention by the head office is destructive to incentive systems built upon
profit centers, Rutenberg comments:

> Whether maneuvering is worth the effort
> can be determined only by building a
> model; the difference between current
> costs and model optimal costs provides
> a benchmark against which to judge the
> behavioral costs of headquarters in-
> tervention.[49]

Rutenberg's is only a partial analysis for
strategic planning because it assumes as given the
planned operations of each subsidiary and, in particular, those subsidiaries that will be net sources
or recipients of corporate funds. Because his is a
deterministic model, it does not deal with anticipated risks such as currency controls, exchange
fluctuations, and expropriations. Since the risk
factor often determines the transfer pricing system in international business, Rutenberg's model is
not too applicable. However, his point is well
taken that "formally" planning for optimal flexibility in the face of risk ought to wait until there
is more data and experience with a deterministic
model.[50] Rutenberg's model has provided an excellent beginning, but until it is modified to handle
the inherent risks in international business, it
cannot be of much use for actual multinational
business operations.

International Studies

There have been three major studies of U.S.
systems of international transfer pricing. The
most comprehensive one was done by Business International Corporation.[51] Its overall report was
concerned with "how international companies can

---

includes the pricing of management services and intracorporate loans (these items are included in the
definition of "transfer pricing" in this study).

approach the task of establishing unified corporate
pricing policies and procedures for foreign operations, and what success or failure other firms have
met in trying to resolve the problems that are common to all firms."[52]

The firms that participated in the study set
out seven essentials for an effective system.[53]
The transfer pricing system must:

1. Provide a fair profit to the producing
unit;

2. Enable the purchasing unit to meet profit
targets despite the pressure of competitive prices;

3. Permit top management to compare and evaluate the performance of corporate units;

4. Reduce the executive time spent on pricing
decisions and mediation of intercorporate pricing
disputes;

5. Establish a transfer price acceptable to
national tax authorities;

6. Set a transfer price acceptable to national
customs officials for duty valuation purposes;

7. Provide control over the pricing practices
of foreign subsidiaries to ensure that profit goals
are met.

The firms also agreed that there were essentially only four system orientations and that the
choice was a function of a firm's product line, distribution channels, sales margins, degree of ownership in foreign operations, and the scope of the
foreign operations. The four orientations were:

1. Transfers at arm's-length or established
market prices to independent customers.

2. Transfers at negotiated prices among corporate units.

3.   Transfers at local manufacturing cost plus a standard markup.

4.   Transfers at the local manufacturing cost of the most efficient corporate unit plus a standard markup.

The researchers pointed out that no single system seemed capable of meeting all possible difficulties, and this had resulted in the use of multiple systems by most firms. Because of the enormous complexity of administering such a system and the greater attention paid by United States tax officials to intracorporate prices, many multinational firms were adopting a single pricing formula to cover all intracorporate transfers.* The study reported a distinct preference for transfer prices based on methods 3 and 4 cited above.

The advantages mentioned by those using the local-cost-plus-fixed-percentage method were that it placed all units on the same profit basis when they sold to related units, and that it boosted morale by putting the same margin on intracorporate sales by any producing subsidiary. The disadvantages were that it did not create an incentive to reduce costs and that it often left too slim a profit margin for the final selling unit.

Those firms that based their transfer prices on the cost of the most efficient producer in the corporate group said that the big advantage was greater control. This system also placed greater pressure on managers to reduce production costs, because any reduction automatically resulted in additional profit on intracorporate sales.

————————————

*Other factors cited as influencing this trend were (1) the movement toward rationalization of production and interchange of parts, components, and finished goods among subsidiaries in regional trade blocks, and (2) the shift toward distribution through sales subsidiaries rather than through independent subsidiaries.

However, neither system solved the basic problem of deciding what should constitute cost or what the fixed percentage markup should be: Should research and development costs be allocated? Should overhead variances be charged? How much of a profit markup is optimal?

One conclusion of the study was that the division-of-net-income approach might replace these cost-plus formulas as the most acceptable pricing basis for national revenue services, thereby eliminating the greatest weakness of the cost-plus systems (failure to relate the transfer price to the final price in the marketplace) and the need to determine cost allocations.

Based on the experiences of the 30 firms interviewed by Business International Corporation, the final analysis yielded the following generalizations:[54]

1. When transfers are made between wholly owned subsidiaries and between the parent company and these subsidiaries, a formula pricing arrangement based on a fixed markup from either local production costs or the cost of the most efficient producer in the corporate group seems to be the best answer.

2. When joint venture companies are involved, an arm's-length pricing formula seems best, since it preserves a maximum of profit on export sales by the U.S. parent to these companies and reduces the area of conflict over pricing that could arise with the local partner.

3. Arm's-length prices are difficult to estimate in many cases, but they can be based on the distributor price with an adjustment for the marketing and service functions performed by the joint venture company.

4. Cost is a difficult concept to define, but generally intercorporate transfers are based on

factory costs (standard cost plus variation) with a
burden rate for factory overhead applied. General
corporate expenses are picked up in most cases
through management contracts, and research and development costs are recaptured through licensing
agreements with the subsidiaries.

5. The markup from cost for wholly owned subsidiaries is normally based on the domestic industry
average or on the total manufacturing sales margin
for all firms. However, this may not be satisfactory for international sales, and some adjustment
may be necessary to maximize the profit opportunities of all producing and selling units in all markets. One simple alternative is to establish a
very low markup, allowing all selling units to work
with a reasonable margin. This may result in tax
and customs difficulties, however.

6. A division-of-net-income approach elimi-
nates the need to justify many cost, markup, and
allocation of overhead and research and development
determinations used by the firm to the national
revenue service, since profit rather than the com-
ponent parts of profit becomes the determining factor. The net income approach has the added advantage of recognizing the necessity of leaving a
reasonable profit in the marketing company for competitive maneuvering.

7. Tax considerations in pricing are important
but should not be valued above sound business practice and the needs of the manufacturing and marketing organizations, including the need to preserve
high morale in all corporate units by giving them
profit recognition for their efforts.

8. One corporate group may find it necessary
to utilize several pricing arrangements depending
on the ownership patterns of its foreign units, the
type of customer to which the final product will be
sold, and whether the corporate customer is a sales
or manufacturing unit. And in some cases, there
may be unusual product characteristics that will
call for the use of differing pricing structures.

The Business International study did not solve
the transfer pricing problem. It only presented
alternatives to consider, the strengths and weak-
nesses of each alternative, and the experiences of
firms in following these several courses of action.
The report strongly suggested that there is no general solution--only a rational framework of analysis.

James Shulman was the one who identified and
analyzed the major environmental variables unique
to transfer pricing in international business.[55]
He discussed at length the problems caused by dif-
ferential income taxes, customs duties, currency
fluctuations, economic restrictions, government and
economic instability, expropriation, foreign financial standings, competition, foreign partners, and
antitrust laws.

The identification of these problem areas and
the various methods used to circumvent them came
from the interviews Shulman conducted with eight
U.S. multinational firms. Only a few firms considered all of these problems when formulating
their transfer prices. Taxes received the most
attention and were treated as the most important
factor. Shulman's criteria for transfer pricing
stemmed from two basic premises:[56]

1. The need of a multinational corporation
for a feasible control system is rendered more ur-
gent by the additional complexities of a larger
environment.

2. Any actions that affect the control mechan-
ism are likely to be more dangerous to the firm engaged in multinational business. When new adapta-
tions to new conditions cause alterations to an existing system, management must be careful not merely
to substitute one problem for another.

Based on these premises, Shulman's criteria
were as follows:[57]

1. Transfer pricing should not cause alterations to an existing system of control unless

adequate adjustments compensate for the change and keep the system operational.

2. Transfer pricing systems must be compatible with the operational goals of the control system and must reinforce its regulatory functions.

3. When external conditions are of such substance that they either expose the firm to grave threats or make available opportunities for material gains, the transfer pricing system must be capable of being revamped or the control system altered.

Shulman characterized the actual transfer pricing systems of his firms as having either a cost or market orientation. His sample was too small to draw any significance from the breakdown. His argument was well stated though that where a true external market for the product does not exist or where strong central control is desirable, a cost-based system will more closely fulfill corporate goals.[58]

The Conference Board Record conducted a survey of its panel of senior U.S. international executives, representing 130 corporations, on policies and procedures used in conducting commercial relations with foreign subsidiaries and other controlled units abroad.[59] For the majority of respondents, the transfer of goods to controlled units overseas was the most important aspect of their commercial relations with these units. U.S. tax policies were listed as a major determinant of transfer prices; however, the paramount consideration was the overall impact on the consolidated profit so that profit was taken where it was best for the total corporation.

Transfer prices were most commonly established either on a cost-plus basis or by negotiation. The deciding factor appeared to be the availability from an outside source of the product being transferred. They carefully pointed out that definitions of "cost" varied considerably. Some included administrative expenses, others included these plus an allocation of profit, and some meant the full cost

(research and development, overhead, all expenses,
but no profit).

None of these studies established a definitive
case for a particular orientation or even suggested
that there is one. They did provide data for comparison, however, by identifying the major variables
and parameters that are considered by U.S. multinational firms in formulating their transfer prices.
With these data as a basis for comparison, the present study was conducted.

SUMMARY

After four decades of research, the problem of
international transfer pricing has not yet been
solved, and prospects for a solution seem dim. The
corporate goals of firms are so diverse and the international environment so complex and metamorphic
that no single system works equally well for all
firms at any given time, or even for one firm over
time.

Neither domestic theory nor its application
provides an answer. There is no international theory or even consensus among the multinational firms.
One can only allude to a potential resolution being
forced upon firms by an exogenous force such as
local governments. By investigating the non-U.S.
systems of international transfer pricing, this researcher has gained some new information and experience that point to a solution.

NOTES

1. For excellent theoretical treatments and
discussions, see Gordon Shillinglaw, Cost Account-
ing: Analysis and Control (Homewood, Ill.: Richard
D. Irwin, 1967), Chapter 17; Charles Horngren, Cost
Accounting (Englewood Cliffs, N.J.: Prentice-Hall,
1967), pp. 348-54; and Carl Moore and Robert
Jaedicke, Managerial Accounting (Cincinnati, Ohio:
South-Western, 1967), pp. 597-609.

For lesser treatments, see R. W. Schattke,
H. G. Jensen, and V. L. Bean, Accounting: Concepts
and Uses (Boston: Allyn and Bacon, 1969), pp. 616-
20; Adolph Matz, Curry Othel, and George Frank, Cost
Accounting (Cincinnati, Ohio: South-Western, 1967),
pp. 929-32; Robert Anthony, Management Accounting
(Homewood, Ill.: Richard D. Irwin, 1970), pp. 428-
29; Myron Gordon and Gordon Shillinglaw, Accounting:
A Managerial Approach (Homewood, Ill.: Richard D.
Irwin, 1967), pp. 656-57; R. L. Dixon, S. R. Hepworth,
and W. A. Paton, Essentials of Accounting (New York:
Macmillan, 1966), pp. 448-49; and M. Backer and L.
Jacobsen, Cost Accounting (New York: McGraw-Hill,
1964).

2.   David Solomons, Divisional Performance,
Management and Control (New York: Research Foundation of Financial Executives Institute, 1965).

3.   R. N. Anthony, John Dearden, and R. F.
Vancil, Management Control Systems (Homewood, Ill.:
Richard D. Irwin, 1965), pp. 251-75.

4.   For the best discussions, see Endel Kolde,
International Business Enterprise (Englewood Cliffs,
N.J.: Prentice-Hall, 1968), Chapter 27; John Hess
and Philip Cateora, International Marketing (Home-
wood, Ill.: Richard D. Irwin, 1966), Chapter 19;
and David Zenoff and Jack Zwick, International Fi-
nancial Management (Englewood Cliffs, N.J.:
Prentice-Hall, 1969), pp. 424-30.
Other good treatments include those by Virgil
Salera, Multinational Business (Boston: Houghton
Mifflin, 1969); Raymond Vernon, Manager in the In-
ternational Economy (Englewood Cliffs, N.J.:
Prentice-Hall, 1968); and Richard Robinson, International Management (New York: Holt, Rinehart, and
Winston, 1967).

5.   See E. A. Camman, "Interdepartmental
Profits," Journal of Accountancy, XLVIII (1929),
37-44; and National Association of Cost Accountants,
"Interdepartment and Interbranch Transfers," 1930
Yearbook, p. 206.

6. H. N. Broom, "Method of Accounting for Interdepartmental Profits," Accounting Review, XXIII, 4 (October 1948), 417-20.

7. See Paul Cook, "Decentralization and the Transfer Pricing Problem," Journal of Business, XXVIII, 2 (April 1955), 87-94; and Joel Dean, "Decentralization and Intracompany Pricing," Harvard Business Review, XXXIII, 4 (July-August 1955), 65-74.

8. Jack Hirschleifer, "On the Economics of Transfer Pricing," Journal of Business, XXIX, 3 (July 1956), 172-84, and "Economics of a Divisionalized Firm," Journal of Business, XXX, 3 (April 1957), 96-108.

9. Paul Cook, "New Techniques for Intracompany Pricing," Harvard Business Review, XXXV, 4 (July-August 1957), 74-81; and Harold Bierman, "Pricing Intracompany Transfer," Accounting Review, XXXIV, 3 (July 1959), 429-32.

10. See particularly John Dearden, "Interdivisional Pricing," Harvard Business Review, XXXVIII, 1 (January-February 1960), 117-25; Gordon Shillinglaw, "Toward a Theory of Income Measurement," Accounting Review, XXXVII, 2 (April 1962), 208-16; R. Boyd, "Transfer Prices and Profitability Measurement," The Controller, XXIX, 2 (February 1961); John Dearden, "The Case of the Disputing Divisions: How Should Decentralized Organizations Handle the Interdivisional Pricing Problem?" Harvard Business Review, XLII, 3 (June 1964), 158-59; Jean P. Boyer, "Intercompany Pricing's Effect on R.O.I. Analysis, Financial Executive, XXXII, 12 (December 1964), 20-26; J. J. Mauriel and R. N. Anthony, "Misevaluation of Investment Center Performance," Harvard Business Review, XLIV, 4 (March-April 1966), 98-105; James Fremgen, "Measuring the Profit of Part of a Firm," Management Accounting, XLVII, 5 (1) (January 1966), 26-29; Martin Cohen, "Intercorporate Transactions and Consolidated Returns," Journal of Accountancy, CXXI, 4 (April 1966), 50-56; and Harold Bierman, Topics in Accounting (New York: McGraw-Hill, 1963).

11. See Howard Greer, "Divisional Profit Calculation--Notes on the Transfer Pricing Problem," NAA Bulletin, XLIII, 1 (July 1962), 5-12; Robert McLain, "Transfer Pricing Can Contribute to Divisional Profit Performance," NAA Bulletin, XLIV, 1 (August 1963), 29-32; W. J. Riley, "Processing Interunit Transfers," NAA Bulletin, XLVI, 2 (August 1965), 43-45; and D. H. Li, "International Pricing," NAA Bulletin, XLVI, 2 (June 1965), 51-54.

12. Nicholas Dopuch and David Drake, "Accounting Problems of Mathematical Programming Approach to the Transfer Price Problem," Journal of Accounting Research, II, 1 (Spring 1964), 10-25.

13. J. R. Gould, "Internal Pricing in a Firm Where There Are Costs of Using an Outside Market," Journal of Business, XXXVII, 1 (January 1964), 61-67.

14. Willard Stone, "Legal Implications of Intracorporate Pricing," Accounting Review, XXXIX, 1 (January 1964), 38-42.

15. Charles Horngren, Cost Accounting (Englewood Cliffs, N.J.: Prentice-Hall, 1962).

16. For earlier treatments, see C. B. Nickerson, Managerial Cost Accounting (New York: McGraw-Hill, 1954); R. N. Anthony, Managerial Accounting (Homewood, Ill.: Richard D. Irwin, 1960); George Husband, Accounting: Administrative and Financial (Philadelphia: Chilton, 1960); and M. Gordon and G. Shillinglaw, Accounting: A Managerial Approach (Homewood, Ill.: Richard D. Irwin, 1962).

17. James Shulman, "Transfer Pricing in Multinational Business" (unpublished Ph.D. dissertation, Harvard University, 1966).

18. Business International Corporation, Solving International Pricing Problems (New York: the Corporation, 1965).

19. There were two pre-1965 articles on taxes, one by H. Stitt and J. Conner, "International

Intercompany Pricing," <u>Canadian Tax Journal</u> (May
1962); and one by Willard Stone, "Tax Considerations
in Intracompany Pricing," <u>Accounting Review</u>, XXXV, 1
(January 1960), 45-50.

20. These include Harry Mansfield, "The Proposed 482 Regs: The Problems with Which Practition-
ers Will Have to Contend"; Sheldon Cohen, "How the
I.R.S. Intends to Administer the New Regulations
under Section 482"; and Stanley Surrey, "Treasury's
Need to Curb Tax Avoidance in Foreign Business
through the Use of 482."
     Other thorough treatments of the tax law change
are those by Paul Seghers, "Pricing U.S. Manufactured
Goods Sold to Subsidiaries for Sale to Customers
Abroad," <u>Taxes</u>, XLIV, 2 (February 1966), 97-101;
Walter F. O'Connor, "Can Intercompany Pricing Arrangements Avoid Being Upset by Section 482?" <u>Journal of
Taxation</u>, XXVI, 5 (May 1967), 262-68; Robert Holzman,
"IRS Amplifies the Rules for Intercompany Transactions," <u>Management Review</u>, LVII, 7 (July 1968), 37-
41, and "A Critique of IRS Arm's-Length Concept,"
<u>Journal of Accountancy</u>, CXXVI, 5 (November 1968),
50-53; James Eustice, "Review of Section 482," <u>Tax
Review</u> (Spring 1968); D. Cook, "Interunit Pricing
and Your New Pricing Expert: IRS," <u>Management Ac-
counting</u>, LI, 2 (August 1969), 9-11; Paul Seghers,
"Intercompany Pricing vs. Section 482," <u>Business
Abroad</u>, XCIV, 11 (November 1969), 49-50, and "How
to Set and Defend Intercompany Prices under Section
482 Regulations," <u>Taxes</u>, XLVII, 4 (October 1969),
606-12; and Warren Keegen, "Multinational Pricing:
How Far Is Arm's Length?" <u>Columbia Journal of World
Business</u>, IV, 3 (May-June 1969), 57-66.

21. See, in particular, John Walter's article,
"The Eli Lilly Decision," <u>Taxes</u>, XLIV, 2 (February
1966), 622-24; and Paul Seghers' article, "Eli Lilly
Case Points to a Defense against IRS Intercompany
Pricing Suits," <u>Business Abroad</u>, XCII, 10 (May 15,
1967), 21. The Business International Corporation's
study, <u>Solving International Pricing Problems</u>, also
has an excellent discussion of the Lilly Case.

22. Joseph Wodjak, "An Introduction to the Ex-
ternal Aspects of Transfer Pricing," New York C.P.A.,
XXXVIII, 5 (May 1968), 341-52; and Andrew Philippakas
and Howard Thompson, "Reward Functions, Transfer
Prices and Decentralization," Quarterly Review of
Economics and Business, X, 1 (Spring 1970), 57-66.

23. See James Shulman, "When the Price is
Wrong by Design," Columbia Journal of World Business, II, 3 (May-June 1967), 69-77.

24. James Greene, "Intercorporate Pricing
across National Frontiers," Conference Board Record,
VI, 10 (October 1969).

25. H. M. Schoenfeld, "Some Special Accounting Problems of Multinational Enterprises," Management International Review, IX, 4-5 (1969), 3-11.

26. Hirschleifer, "On the Economics of Transfer Pricing."

27. Philippakas and Thompson, "Reward Functions, Transfer Prices and Decentralization."

28. Solomons, Divisional Performance, Management and Control.

29. Gould, "Internal Pricing in a Firm Where
There Are Costs of Using an Outside Market."

30. For information on the decomposition principle, see G. B. Dantzig and P. Wolfe, "Decomposition Principle for Linear Programs," Operations Research, VIII (January-February 1960), 101-11, and a
related article in Econometrica, XXIX (October 1961),
767-78. For good treatments of shadow prices and
linear programming applications, see R. Dorfman,
P. Samuelson, and R. Solow, Linear Programming and
Economic Analysis (New York: McGraw-Hill, 1958);
George Hadley, Linear Programming (Reading, Mass.:
Addison-Wesley, 1962), particularly Chapter 11;
Philip Wolfe, "Recent Developments in Non-Linear

Programming," the Rand Corporation R-401-Pr (May 1962); and George Dantzig, Linear Programming and Extensions (Princeton, N.J.: Princeton University Press, 1963), particularly Chapter 23.

31. Dopuch and Drake, "Accounting Problems of Mathematical Programming Approach to the Transfer Price Problem."

32. Dean, "Decentralization and Intracompany Pricing," p. 73.

33. Dearden, "Interdivisional Pricing," p. 124.

34. Cook, "Decentralization and the Transfer Pricing Problem," p. 94, and Wodjak, "An Introduction to the External Aspects of Transfer Pricing," p. 351.

35. Frederick Finney, "Pricing Interdivisional Transfers," Management Accounting, XLVIII, 3, Sect. 1 (November 1966), pp. 10-20.

36. Hirschleifer, "On the Economics of Transfer Pricing," p. 172.

37. Fremgen, "Measuring the Profit of Part of a Firm," p. 28.

38. Bierman, "Pricing Intracompany Transfer," p. 430.

39. Curiously enough, these conditions were initially laid down in the first article on transfer pricing (Paul Cook's article in 1955, "Decentralization and the Transfer Pricing Problem," Accounting Review, XXXV [January 1960], 88).

40. See Stone, "Tax Considerations in Intracompany Pricing," pp. 45-48.

41. Court of Claims, February 17, 1967 (67-1 USTC 372F 2d 990).

42. See Wojdak, "An Introduction to the External Aspects of Transfer Pricing," pp. 346-49.

43. See Stone, "Legal Implications of Intracompany Pricing," p. 41.

44. National Industrial Conference Board, "Interdivisional Transfer-Pricing," Studies in Business Policy, No. 122 (1967).

45. Willard Stone, "Management Practices with Respect to Internal Transfer Pricing in Large Manufacturing Companies" (unpublished Ph.D. dissertation, University of Pennsylvania, 1957).

46. By "cost-plus," he means the full manufactured cost plus an allowance for profit; see Keegen, "Multinational Pricing," p. 66.

47. See Cook, "New Techniques for Intracompany Pricing," p. 75.

48. David P. Rutenberg, "Maneuvering Liquid Assets in a Multinational Company: Formulation and Deterministic Solution Procedures," Management Science, XVI, 10 (June 1970), 671-84.

49. Ibid., p. 672.

50. Ibid.

51. Business International Corporation, Solving International Pricing Problems.

52. Ibid., p. 1.

53. Ibid., p. 18.

54. Ibid., p. 31.

55. Shulman, "Transfer Pricing in Multinational Business."

56. Ibid., p. 138.

57. Ibid., p. 139.

58. Conversely, he argued that where profit centers are utilized and are accompanied by real delegation of authority over access to markets, sources and overproduction decisions, and where a true market environment exists, a market-oriented transfer pricing system will be better. See ibid., pp. 143-44.

59. See Greene, "Intercorporate Pricing across National Frontiers," pp. 43-48.

INTRODUCTION

Research designs differ in accordance with the purpose of a study. Claire Selltiz et al. place research purposes into four broad groupings:[1]

> (1) to gain familiarity with a phenomenon or to achieve new insights into it, often in order to formulate a more precise research problem or to develop further hypotheses; (2) to portray accurately the characteristics of a particular individual, situation, or group; (3) to determine the frequency with which something occurs or with which it is associated with something else; and (4) to test a hypothesis of a causal relationship between variables.

Studies that emphasize the discovery of ideas and insights (the first purpose listed above) are generally called "formulative," "exploratory," or "pioneering" studies. They require a research design "flexible enough to permit the consideration of many different aspects of a phenomenon."[2] Such

studies are appropriate for investigating problems
about which there is little or no knowledge.

Studies with the second and third purposes
have similar research design requirements, for they
emphasize accuracy. The design must minimize bias
and maximize the reliability of the evidence col-
lected.

Studies that test causal hypotheses require a
research design that not only reduces bias and maxi-
mizes reliability but also permits inferences about
causality. Experimentation is especially suited
for these studies although many of them do not take
this form.

As Selltiz et al. point out, different types
of studies are not always sharply distinguishable,
and any given piece of research may contain ele-
ments of two or more of the purposes listed. However, since the primary emphasis of any single
study is usually on only one function, the research
design should be selected accordingly.

Certain research techniques have been developed
for each type of study. The more a problem is precisely defined, the more sophisticated will be the
tools that can be used. For testing causal hypotheses, for example, one can use parametric or non-
parametric tests, "t-tests," "F-tests," Spearman
rank-order correlation tests, X^2 tests, tests of
auto and serial correlation, Pearsonian "r" tests
that measure the linear correlation between two
variables, and many others.[3] There are also many
sociometric scales and indexes that can be used in
attitudinal studies of all types.[4]

Most of these techniques, although excellent,
are not applicable to exploratory studies such as
this one. Formulative studies must rely on more
biased observations, fewer quantifiable measures,
and more unstructured design; this does not mean
that they are any less valuable--only less precise.
To date research in international business has

largely been either exploratory or descriptive.
Past contributions have been important, even though
many of their conclusions are not statistically sup-
portable due to the complexity of the problems.   If
the research design and techniques of this study
are imprecise, it is only because the nature of the
problem does not lend itself to greater precision.

Transfer pricing is not only extremely complex
but very secretive.   It could not be expected that
there would be much voluntary participation in an
outsider's study of a confidential matter.   A less
than statistically significant degree of response
does not lessen the importance of the topic; it
only means that there must be additional flexibility in the research design and that caution must be
used in drawing inferences from the study's findings.   This chapter will discuss the research method
utilized and evaluate its appropriateness and success.

The major objective of this research was to make
a pioneering study of non-U.S. systems of international intracorporate pricing by comparing their systems, attitudes, and experiences with those of their
U.S. counterparts.   Information about U.S. corporations was obtained solely from the available literature.   Information about the non-U.S. corporations
was secured through correspondence and interviews.*

The general procedure was as follows: A search
was made of the literature to identify the major
types of systems, viewpoints, and problems related
to international transfer pricing; this information
was used as background for comparison.   Then a list
of non-U.S. corporations with interest or control
in U.S. manufacturing companies was obtained from
the U.S. Department of Commerce.[5]   This list provided the names of the parents, those of their U.S.
subsidiaries, the degree of ownership, and the type

---

*Correspondence and interviews are the two
most commonly used techniques for exploratory and
descriptive studies.

of goods being produced. From the 412 non-U.S. corporations listed, only those with wholly owned subsidiaries were selected. The addresses of the subsidiaries and the names of their executive officers
were obtained largely from industrial and financial
indexes; in some cases they were secured from appropriate national embassies. Direct correspondence was
then initiated with the U.S. subsidiaries. Their
replies were analyzed and subsequently discussed
with partners of eight international accounting
firms. The partners were also asked to comment on
national similarities and differences in light of
their own personal experience.

The literature search, the interviews and correspondence with the firms, and the discussions with
the international accountants constituted the essential data for this study.

FIELD RESEARCH TECHNIQUE

Population

The population consisted of 412 non-U.S. firms,
representing 15 different countries, with a total
of 646 U.S. subsidiaries.* Table 1 shows the
country-company-subsidiary breakdown for both the
population and the sample.

Foreign investment in the United States is predominantly Western European and Canadian. Three-
fourths of all subsidiaries are at least partially
owned by corporations in these geographic areas.
The biggest single investors are England, Canada,
and West Germany, whose U.S. subsidiaries comprise
63 percent of the total. The only non-Western foreign investor is Japan, whose 21 companies control
22 U.S. manufacturing subsidiaries. Most of the
other Japanese investments in the United States are
in such natural resources as lumber and fisheries.

---

*This total does not include the gasoline sta-
tions owned by the non-U.S. oil companies.

TABLE 1

Population and Sample Breakdown by Countries and Companies

Country	Population		Sample	
	No. of Foreign Companies	No. of U.S. Subsidiaries	No. of Foreign Companies	No. of Wholly Owned Subsidiaries
Australia	2	3	2	3
Belgium	9	17	8	14
Canada	114	150	27	137
Denmark	6	6	6	6
England	107	169	39	136
Finland	1	1	1	1
France	25	38	6	25
Italy	5	6	3	6
Japan	21	22	6	15
Netherlands	19	67	8	55
Netherlands Antilles	1	8	1	7
Norway	1	1	1	1
Sweden	20	26	11	24
Switzerland	19	32	10	25
West Germany	62	100	17	77
Total	412	646	145	532

By the end of 1968, manufacturing and petroleum interests comprised nearly two-thirds of the total value of direct foreign investment in the United States.[6] More than 80 percent of the foreign investment earnings in 1968 went to companies located in England, Canada, the Netherlands, and Switzerland.[7]

The Sample

The Department of Commerce publication listed the names of all firms with any interest or control in U.S. manufacturing companies. The sample used in this study, however, included only those firms with wholly owned subsidiaries in the United States. Thus 145 firms were selected, having a total of 532 U.S. subsidiaries.* These subsidiaries manufactured products in 18 different standard industrial categories, as shown in Table 2. Table 3 presents a similar breakdown for each of the 15 countries represented.

A personal letter was sent to an executive in each firm, requesting a list of the environmental variables that are taken into consideration when intracompany prices are being formulated. Each executive was asked to rank each variable in terms of its importance and frequency of consideration. Finally, each executive was asked to comment generally about other systems of which he was aware and about frequently encountered problems and methods used to solve them.

Direct follow-up interviews were conducted with 16 of the respondents. The interviews were arranged after receiving a written invitation from the firms to discuss the topic in greater detail at a mutually convenient time. All of the interviews

---

*See Table 1. In those cases where a parent had more than one U.S. subsidiary, the largest or most representative one was chosen for inclusion in this study.

TABLE 2

Sample Breakdown by Standard
Industrial Classification
(145 firms queried, 60 responded)

	Queried	Responded
Food and kindred products	14	9
Tobacco	2	2
Textile mill products	5	0
Apparel	2	0
Lumber and wood products (except furniture)	3	0
Furniture and fixtures	2	1
Paper and allied products	6	4
Chemicals and allied products	27	10
Petroleum refining and related industries	5	1
Rubber and miscellaneous products	4	2
Stone, clay, glass, and concrete products	2	0
Primary metal industries	7	4
Fabricated metal products	12	5
Machinery (nonelectrical)	26	11
Electrical machinery, equipment, and supplies	13	5
Transportation equipment	3	3
Professional, scientific, and controlling instruments; photographic and optical goods; watches and clocks	6	1
Miscellaneous manufacturing industries	6	2

TABLE 3

Sample Breakdown by Country and Product Classification

Country	No. of Firms Queried	Apparel Q	Apparel R	Petroleum Q	Petroleum R	Rubber and Plastics Q	Rubber and Plastics R	Primary Metals Q	Primary Metals R	Fabricated Metals Q	Fabricated Metals R	Food Q	Food R	Chemicals Q	Chemicals R	Paper Products Q	Paper Products R
Australia	2	1	0	-	-	-	-	-	-	-	-	-	-	-	-	-	-
Belgium	8	-	-	1	0	2	1	1	0	2	1	-	-	-	-	-	-
Canada	31	-	-	2	1	-	-	4	2	1	1	6	5	-	-	3	2
Denmark	6	-	-	-	-	-	-	-	-	-	-	2	1	1	0	-	-
England	39	1	0	1	0	1	1	1	1	2	1	3	1	6	2	3	2
Finland	1	-	-	-	-	-	-	-	-	-	-	-	-	-	-	-	-
France	6	-	-	-	-	-	-	-	-	-	-	-	-	3	2	-	-
Italy	3	-	-	-	-	-	-	-	-	-	-	1	1	-	-	-	-
Japan	6	-	-	-	-	-	-	-	-	-	-	-	-	-	-	-	-
Netherlands	8	-	-	1	0	-	-	-	-	2	0	-	-	4	0	-	-
Netherlands Antilles	1	-	-	-	-	-	-	-	-	-	-	-	-	-	-	-	-
Sweden	10	-	-	-	-	-	-	1	1	1	0	2	1	2	2	-	-
Switzerland	10	-	-	-	-	-	-	-	-	1	0	-	-	6	1	-	-
West Germany	17	-	-	-	-	1	0	-	-	3	2	-	-	5	3	-	-

54

Country	Stone, Clay, Glass, Concrete		Electrical Machinery		Nonelec. Machinery		Wood		Transportation		Scientific Equipment		Furniture		Textiles		Tobacco		Miscellaneous	
	Q	R	Q	R	Q	R	Q	R	Q	R	Q	R	Q	R	Q	R	Q	R	Q	R
Australia	-	-	-	-	-	-	-	-	-	-	-	-	-	-	-	-	-	-	1	0
Belgium	-	-	1	0	1	1	-	-	-	-	-	-	-	-	-	-	-	-	-	-
Canada	-	-	4	2	5	3	1	0	-	-	-	-	1	1	1	0	-	-	-	-
Denmark	-	-	-	-	1	1	-	-	1	1	-	-	-	-	-	-	-	-	1	0
England	1	0	3	1	7	2	1	0	-	-	1	1	-	-	4	0	2	2	2	1
Finland	-	-	-	-	1	0	-	-	-	-	-	-	-	-	-	-	-	-	-	-
France	1	0	2	1	-	-	-	-	-	-	-	-	-	-	-	-	-	-	-	-
Italy	-	-	1	1	1	1	-	-	-	-	-	-	-	-	-	-	-	-	-	-
Japan	-	-	1	0	1	0	-	-	-	-	2	0	1	0	-	-	-	-	1	0
Netherlands	-	-	-	-	-	-	-	-	-	-	-	-	-	-	-	-	-	-	1	1
Netherlands Antilles	-	-	-	-	-	-	-	-	1	1	1	0	-	-	-	-	-	-	-	-
Sweden	-	-	-	-	5	2	-	-	1	1	-	-	-	-	-	-	-	-	-	-
Switzerland	-	-	-	-	1	0	-	-	-	-	-	-	-	-	-	-	-	-	-	-
West Germany	-	-	1	1	3	1	1	0	1	1	2	0	-	-	-	-	-	-	-	-

Note: "Q" stands for queried; "R," for responded.

55

were held with corporate officials at the offices
of the U.S. subsidiaries. A second letter was sent
to each of the 16 executives before the interview
with a list of questions to be discussed during the
meeting. The questions were phrased in such a way
to permit the executives to organize their thoughts
and formulate their answers. The letter also included a summary of the variables and constraints
that are considered important by U.S. firms, as suggested in the literature. It was hoped that the
summary would elicit comparisons. The executives
were also asked to comment on general trends in international transfer pricing in terms of complexity,
orientation, and relative importance.

Essentially the same approach was used when interviewing the international accounting partners.
The major difference was that they also received
some of the preliminary findings from the research
on the non-U.S. multinational firms. Each international accounting firm decided which partner
would be available for interviewing; in most cases
it was the senior international partner, but occasionally it was his assistant. The data obtained
from the subsidiary executives and the accounting
firms' partners were combined, analyzed, and then
resubmitted to the partners for final comments.

EVALUATION

Quantity of Information Received

Written replies were received from 60 of the
145 companies--a response rate of 41 percent. This
percentage, although not high, was actually somewhat higher than anticipated. Transfer pricing is
an extremely sensitive and secretive area for all
firms, especially multinational firms. This is
partly due to the increase in investigations and
litigation by national government agencies, and the
growing concern shown by other groups inside and
outside the firm. Management, therefore, is not
inclined to discuss transfer pricing openly with an

outsider. Although some persons felt that this
study could not succeed because of the lack of cooperation from various firms, this did not prove to
be the case. Management decided to cooperate because of the importance of transfer pricing, their
hope for help through research, and the pledge of
anonymity.*

Certain geographic and industrial groups were
less cooperative than others. None of the oil companies responded, nor did any of the Japanese or
Swiss firms. Their lack of cooperation was disap-
pointing although not surprising. Historically the
international oil companies have encountered the
most trouble with transfer pricing, and they are
believed to be the biggest abusers. Shortly before
this study was undertaken, the Japanese had been investigated for alleged dumping violations (made possible, at least in principle, by underpricing intracompany transfers), while Swiss businesses are tra-
ditionally secretive about their finances.

More reliable conclusions could have been made
about cultural and industrial patterns if more firms
had participated. However, the international accounting firms provided some useful information,
for most of the firms that did not respond were
their clients. The experience and knowledge of the
accounting firms strengthened this researcher's generalizations about industrial and cultural patterns;
these would have been difficult to justify statistically otherwise.

Quality of the Responses

The quality of the written responses varied
considerably. Some firms wrote several pages of
comments, and others only a few sentences. Several
firms discussed other companies' systems, and many
related experiences encountered by other firms.

---

*These were the factors most often cited by
the participants.

The length of the letter was directly related to
the firm's transfer pricing system. Those that employed market-oriented systems wrote very short letters; those with cost-based systems wrote rather
lengthy letters. This relationship was probably
due to the fact that very little justification is
needed for using market prices, while considerably
more is needed for cost-based systems.

In general the written responses were straight-
forward and helpful. Any ambiguities were cleared
up by additional correspondence or telephone conver-
sations. Eight firms said that they were unable to
discuss transfer pricing with outsiders, and so no
further correspondence was conducted with them.

The information obtained through personal interviews was the most helpful and enlightening.
The executives and partners were extremely candid
in their views and provided several times as much
data as that secured from correspondence. Their
professional caliber, overall knowledge, and cooperation was excellent.

Reliability of the Information Received

The reliability of any information received
about a secretive matter is questionable, particularly when no coercive force or legal obligation is
involved. If a firm said that it used only arm's-
length prices for intracompany transfers, the researcher could not check the validity of this statement. Firms may have introduced a bias by reporting
the use of the most uniformly accepted basis and by
not saying that they used manipulated cost-based
prices.

The international accounting firms were consulted specifically to provide a partial check on
the reliability of the multinational firms' replies
as well as to obtain additional information. The
accounting firms could not verify specific statements made by the individual multinational firms,
for their identity was not revealed. But the

accounting firms commented on industry and cultural patterns, largely substantiating the responses of the individual firms.

Since the participating firms were extremely interested in this study and its potential findings, this may have increased the reliability of their responses. For clearly, if the findings of the study are to help them, truthful replies are necessary.

Completeness of the Coverage

This research did not include all non-U.S. multinational firms or all non-U.S. firms with manufacturing subsidiaries in the United States. Those without U.S. subsidiaries were excluded because of time and financial limitations. Those with U.S. subsidiaries that did not choose to participate excluded themselves.

Several other firms may have been left out unintentionally. The list of companies published by the Department of Commerce contained errors of both commission and omission. Several companies replied that they did not have a non-U.S. parent at all, and several said that their foreign parent was not the one listed. Undoubtedly other U.S. firms with foreign parents were not on the list. The compilers of the list acknowledged these possibilities. They obtained their information from various public sources and did not attempt to secure company verification. In spite of these shortcomings, the list was extremely valuable, and the most complete and up-to-date one available.

Appropriateness of the Method

There was much deliberation about the particular research method to be used. Some thought was given to conducting additional research on U.S. multinational companies to provide a better match of information, but then it was decided that past research was adequate. Constraints of time and money were also important factors.

The use of an open-ended letter rather than a
questionnaire was selected for several reasons.
First, a structured questionnaire tends to produce
structured answers. Second, an open-ended letter
appears less formal and mechanistic. With a subject as personal as pricing, a more informal letter
stood a better chance of producing a usable response.
Third, the nature of the topic calls for some rather
free thinking, which is not easily elicited by a
questionnaire. The major disadvantage to the open
letter lies in comparing replies, because a less
structured question brings forth a diversity of answers. Clearly the advantages of the open letter
outweighed the disadvantages.

There was a problem about whether to send the
letters to the parent offices or the U.S. subsidiaries. The reasons for selecting the subsidiaries
have already been discussed earlier* and will not
be repeated here. Possibly some global perspective
was lost by not corresponding with the parent offices, but the subsidiaries' executives were usually
familiar with the global operating procedures of
their firms and were careful to point out any differences in procedures and problems.

Another problem was deciding who within the
firm should receive the letter. It was decided to
address each letter to the top financial officer
whenever possible. Research on U.S. firms had shown
that these executives were usually most responsible
for making the transfer pricing decisions. In several instances the replies came from company presidents; in a few cases the home offices answered after the letter had been forwarded to them. All replies confirmed the fact that transfer pricing was
a high-level executive matter.

Including the international accounting firms
in this study proved to particularly appropriate.
It became evident during the interviews that the

_____

*See page 12.

partners had often discussed transfer pricing with
both the U.S. subsidiaries and their parents. Because they were frequently called in for advice on
transfer pricing, the partners were cognizant of
different problems, systems, and viewpoints.

Drawing Conclusions, Making Inferences

Very few of the conclusions based on the data
are statistically significant. The letter response
rate was low and the number of firms interviewed was
small. Possible biases in the replies and the samp-
ling have already been mentioned as cautions. Care
should be exercised in making any inferences from
the conclusions of this study, for considerably
more information is needed. However, the virtually
uniform agreement reached on this study's conclusions by the international accounting partners does
add credibility.

NOTES

1. Claire Selltiz et al., Research Methods in
Social Relations (New York: Holt, Rinehart and
Winston, 1962), p. 50.

2. Ibid.

3. For an excellent discussion of these techniques, see Delbert Miller, Handbook of Research Design and Social Measurement (New York: David McKay,
1970).

4. Delbert Miller's book also contains excellent descriptions and analyses of these methods.

5. Thomas Pierpoint and Frank Sheaffer, "List
of Foreign Firms with Some Interest/Control in
American Manufacturing Companies" (Washington, D.C.:
Office of International Investment, Bureau of International Commerce, U.S. Department of Commerce, February 1970).

6. Survey of Current Business, XLIX, 10 (October 1969), 36. Of the $10,815 million of investments, manufacturing contributed $4,475 million and petroleum $2,261 million. Finance and insurance investments comprised $2,305 million and "other" $1,774 million.

7. Ibid., p. 34.

4

Earlier chapters discussed the basic nature of the international transfer pricing problem, the scope of this research, and the research efforts of others. This chapter will describe the major findings of this research.

TRADE FLOWS

The flow pattern of goods and services between the non-U.S. parents and their U.S. subsidiaries is largely one way. Subsidiary imports from parents are substantial while exports to parents are minimal. This was true for virtually all firms that responded. This skewed trade pattern contrasts markedly with the predominantly two-way pattern of U.S. multinational firms. It also differs from the trade pattern of the non-U.S. parents with their other (non-U.S.) subsidiaries. Only three firms indicated that they regularly exported goods and services to their non-U.S. parents, while nearly all of them said that their sister subsidiaries in other countries were heavy exporters to the parent.

The reason cited most often for the one-way trade pattern is that U.S. operations are initiated

to serve the U.S. market, and only in rare instances
is it anticipated that they would export to the parent. Putting it somewhat differently, the U.S. subsidiaries are largely market seekers rather than resource or cost-efficiency seekers.* The relative
production cost disadvantage in the United States,
also frequently cited as a reason for the one-way
trade flow, supports this hypothesis. Additional
support comes from an analysis by standard industrial classification, which shows only 26 firms in
primary metal, petroleum, and food-product industries.**

Six subsidiaries said that the parent exports
they receive are related to parent plant capacity
utilization. When capacity utilization is low, exports tend to increase; when high, exports decrease.
None of the managers was pleased with this type of
"warehouse" relationship, especially those who
could not buy outside the corporate family. In
periods of business expansion, this arrangement often leaves them in short supply, while they have to
accept increases in inventories in slack periods.
These six subsidiaries all handle intermediate or
industrial goods and have either German or English
parents.

Twelve subsidiaries reported that virtually no
trade was conducted with their parent in either
direction. No clear pattern emerged by industrial
classification or by nationality. However, if one
characteristic could be singled out to describe
their products, it would be "specialty items."

---

*This terminology and classification system
was developed by W. D. Hogue of Indiana University's
Department of International Business. Mr. Hogue
feels that operating characteristics will be different for each type because each makes different demands on local environments, is exposed to different risks, and performs different functions in
overall corporate operations.

**Out of a total of 145--see Table 2.

This includes goods primarily made to order for a
particular market, such as differentially seasoned
foods, custom-designed equipment, and culturally
attuned cosmetics and toiletries. This "no-trade"
pattern also characterized the parent's relationship with its non-U.S. subsidiaries.

The largest volume of trade is conducted by
subsidiaries that purchase goods from their parents,
and those that both serve as sales outlets for their
companies' products and manufacture goods themselves.
The latter group often import more finished goods
than they make themselves. An example is a French
cosmetics firm that manufactures a perfume in the
United States specifically for the U.S. market and
also imports the full line of company merchandise
that is produced elsewhere. This arrangement allows
them to market the entire product mix to a U.S.
buyer.

The most unusual trade pattern is in the aluminum industry; it is analogous to a Soviet bilateral
trade agreement based on material balances. The
arrangement works as follows: A U.S. subsidiary of
a European aluminum company needs a particular type
of aluminum for use in fabrication. Upon notifica-
tion by the subsidiary, the European parent arranges
for a nonaffiliated U.S.-owned and based aluminum
company to supply the needed material. In return,
the European parent agrees to supply a similar quantity of aluminum to one of the European subsidiaries
of the U.S. corporation. In this manner the transportation costs and delays are minimized, but not
the transfer pricing problem, because the U.S. subsidiary pays its European parent rather than the
U.S. supplier. Thus the European parent still controls the price (and profit) to its U.S. subsidiary.
This trade arrangement is diagramed in Chart 1.
Often no money changes hands between the two parent companies until year's end, while money flows
between the subsidiaries and the parents throughout the year.* In any case the parent retains

---

*If the materials exchanged exactly balance at
year's end, no money changes hands at all between
the two parents.

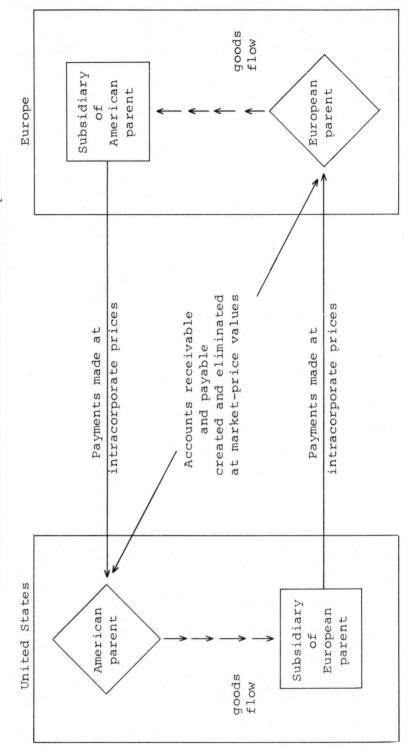

CHART 1

The Trade Pattern of International Aluminum Companies

control even though it does not directly supply the goods.

The accounting firms pointed out that there is a similar "swap" arrangement among firms in the petroleum industry, although none of these firms participated in this study. A local outlet buys from a local refinery (the arrangements being made between the distant parents), but payments are made between each parent and its subsidiary.

DEGREE OF SUBSIDIARY INDEPENDENCE

As a group, U.S. subsidiaries of non-U.S. firms are the most independent subsidiaries in the world. This was the unanimous consensus of the participant firms and the international accountants, and it substantiates the research done by Jean-Luc Rocour.[1] In his study of 59 U.S. subsidiaries of European firms, Rocour concluded that "they represent a unique type of subsidiary and . . . they experience such a degree of independence that many are almost or completely out of the line structure of the parent organization."[2]

This high degree of autonomy is explained by relative differences: the relatively larger size of the U.S. subsidiaries, the relatively higher degree of competition, the relatively faster rate of change, and the relatively tougher legal restrictions in the United States.* Not all subsidiaries are equally autonomous, however; differences exist according to parent nationality.** English- and German-owned subsidiaries are not as independent as the French, Dutch, Canadian, and Belgian; while the Italian- and Scandinavian-owned subsidiaries are the most independent of all. These national

---

*These variables were also mentioned by the firms in Rocour's study.

**Rocour did not identify any national differences.

differences are felt to be a function of a relative
size variable and culturally tied managerial philosophies.

The relative size hypothesis suggests that the
larger the size of the subsidiary relative to its
parent, the more operationally independent it will
be. Thus the higher degree of autonomy possessed
by Italian- and Scandinavian-owned subsidiaries is
due to their size vis-à-vis their parents. The management philosophy hypothesis suggests that some
cultures are more conservative than others, and
that the autonomy of a subsidiary will be a function of the parent country's philosophy. Some interesting ethno-stereotypes emerge from this type
of analysis. English and German managers are viewed
as highly conservative and control-oriented, Italian
managers as freewheeling, and the other managers as
somewhere in between. Self-perceptions of independence coincide with others' perceptions to a considerable degree, although not always for the alleged
reasons. The executives of the English- and German-
owned subsidiaries concede and often bemoan the
tighter degree of control by their parents, while
Italian and Scandinavian managers take great pride
in their independence. Yet all of the executives
agree that they have substantially more freedom
than their counterparts in sister subsidiaries.

In sum, the subsidiary managers feel quite independent, and as a group, the most independent of
subsidiary managers anywhere. They report that they
make the daily and short-run decisions; although
they have a voice in long-range planning, their influence here is much less. They exercise virtually
no influence in the transfer price determination
process.

LOCUS OF TRANSFER PRICE-
DETERMINATION DECISIONS

The setting of transfer prices remains the pre-
rogative of parent company executives. Degrees of

subsidiary participation in their determination
vary, but the bargaining power and final say belong
to the parent.* Of the 16 firms interviewed, 15
feel that their participation is insignificant.
Five of the firms corresponded with replied that
they were totally unaware of how their parent ar-
rives at transfer prices.

The specific persons responsible for setting
intracompany prices are all high-level executives,
regardless of the degree of subsidiary participation or parent nationality. In no firms are the
prices set by an officer lower than a treasurer,
and in many cases, the company presidents are directly responsible. However, it is usually the
chief financial officer of the firm: a vice-
president or a comptroller. Typically the decision
is made by one officer, although in several firms
it may be made by staffs of up to seven people.
Guidelines and policies are set during executive
staff meetings, but within this framework the chief
financial officer is free to operate.

When intracompany sales are infrequent but
large in value, there is substantially more negotiation between the executives of the buying and
the selling firms; the two major financial officers
attempt to work out a mutually satisfactory price.
When disputes arise, the parent company executives
decide the issue. Conflicts are settled in favor
of the subsidiary only in cases where its competitive position would be adversely affected to a significant degree.

The firms that are least dissatisfied with the
one-sidedness of the price determination process
are those that can buy outside the corporate family.

---

*For one firm this is not the case. In this
particular instance, the size of the U.S. subsidiary is double that of its parent, and the comptroller of the U.S. subsidiary sets the transfer
prices.

Three firms mentioned that they were free to buy
from nonaffiliated sources if the internal transfer
price was too high;* otherwise, they were expected
to buy internally. These firms were Italian,
French, and Swedish.

ENVIRONMENTAL VARIABLES CONSIDERED

The nature of competition and the differences
in taxes were cited as the two most important variables taken into account in formulating intracompany
prices. Other variables mentioned were customs duties, export subsidies and tax credits, price controls, inflation, and devaluation.

Nature of the Competition

The degree of competition in the host country
is always an important factor, regardless of how
the initial transfer price is calculated. Usually
no adjustments are made as long as the transfer
price is low enough to keep the subsidiary competitive. A downward adjustment is often made if the
price proposed initially is too high. However, two
firms reported that their parent companies always
charged the maximum price the market would bear.

Competition in the final selling market is not
the only element to consider; there is also competition in the raw materials market, the intermediate
goods market, and the parent company's market. The
widest price range for the good or service being
transferred exists when there is virtually no competition in any of these markets; and there is the
smallest price range for those goods that are sold

---

*This figure is probably too low as an indica-
tor of the practice of permitting outside purchases.
The letter did not ask the firms whether or not
they were allowed to purchase outside, and this may
not have seemed important to respondent subsidiary
managers.

in highly competitive world markets. In the latter
case, the market largely determines the transfer
price. The competitive position of the parent is
especially important when its profits are falling
and need bolstering. Parent profits can be increased by taking the profit on the intracompany
sale in the parent's country rather than abroad.
This can be done by charging the subsidiary at market prices for the goods it buys from the parent.

Tax Considerations

Corporate income tax rates, bases, and laws
comprise the second most frequently cited variable.
Once a competitive position has been attained, many
companies seek to maximize their net world income
by maneuvering their profits to the lowest tax
areas. They exercise considerable care with respect
to particular national tax legislation, such as Section 482, however. No non-U.S. company has been
caught violating Section 482 to date, but some of
them are now facing the threat. Since Germany and
Canada have recently adopted similar regulations,
several German- and Canadian-owned subsidiaries reported that they have changed their corporate transfer pricing policies.

Opportunities for tax avoidance or deferment
are also decreasing as national tax rate differen-
tials decrease. Because tax officials are showing
greater awareness and sophistication, it is more
difficult to use manipulated transfer prices to
lessen tax liabilities. On the whole, therefore,
tax considerations are becoming less important in
setting intracompany prices.

Customs Duties

Many firms no longer think of customs duties
as a major variable. In most cases duties are not
large enough to warrant manipulation of transfer
prices and the resultant possibility of litigation.
It is becoming even more difficult to manipulate suc-
cessfully. Customs officials in several countries

are now assessing duties on equivalent market prices
whenever available, regardless of the invoiced transfer price.*

High duties are often cited as a reason for initiating production in a particular host country, but
these duties become less important after manufacturing has begun. Three firms in the chemical and pharmaceutical industry reported that the volume of
their imports from their parents would increase substantially if U.S. duties were lowered, but that the
transfer prices would not be affected materially because most of the tariffs were based on the U.S.
selling prices rather than on the value of the goods
transferred.

Several firms cited the litigation undertaken
by the United States against several Japanese firms
for alleged dumping violations as ample proof that
it is increasingly difficult to get away with pricing intracompany transfers too low and not worth
the risk.

Export Subsidies

Export subsidies are important to some firms
but quite unimportant to most. The effect of these
subsidies on transfer prices depends on their form.
Transfer prices are set high when a rebate is given
on the value of exports (or the amount of foreign
currency earned), and low if the resulting export
profits are not taxed or are taxed at a lower rate
than other income. These export subsidies are decreasing in importance as they are being phased out
by countries in the European Economic Community.
They remain strongest in the less developed countries, where hard currencies are at a premium.

------

*This finding also emerged in the Business In-
ternational study.

Inflation, Exchange Restrictions,
and Devaluation

Although U.S. subsidiaries do not cite these
variables as major factors in transactions with
their parent companies, the parents take them into
consideration in internal trading with their non-
U.S. subsidiaries. However, the persistently high
rates of inflation in the United States are beginning to change this pattern. With a relatively
higher rate of inflation in the United States, European firms find that they can be more competitive
in U.S. markets by increasing the amount of goods
shipped from Europe to the United States, unless
the U.S. tariffs are based on U.S. selling prices.
Several firms reported that they had made substantial inroads into U.S. markets because of the
cheaper prices obtained from their parents.

Exchange restrictions are an important consideration for non-U.S. trade. If a Brazilian subsidiary can import only a given value amount of material
from the "outside," the parent often underprices the
material. When there are dividend restrictions in
the host country, the parent often uses artificially
inflated transfer prices to get the money out. Thus
non-U.S. companies view their problems in the same
manner and utilize the same techniques to circumvent
them as their U.S. counterparts.

Price controls are important in some countries,
but not in trade with U.S. subsidiaries. A large
English pharmaceutical and sundries manufacturer
remarked that once an import price from the parent
is established, it is virtually impossible to change
it upward. Therefore, transfer prices tend to be on
the high side.

Devaluation and revaluation are important factors for all firms, but they seldom affect normal
transfer pricing decisions. Those companies whose
home country's currency is in danger of devaluation
often build up hard currency reserves by shipping
goods to hard currency country subsidiaries at high

hard currency prices. Several English- and French-
owned subsidiaries reported doing this. Conversely,
several German parents manipulate transfers and
transfer prices to build up Deutsche Mark balances
and decrease other currency balances.

The use of intracompany transfers to hedge often causes unfavorable and dysfunctional conse-
quences for the entire firm. Changes in pricing
policies are likely to be noticed by governments,
may not be defensible or reversible from the government's standpoint, may create conflict within
the organization, and may result in suboptimization
of global operations. It is better to use the forward market to protect against devaluation or provide for revaluation.*

Nationalization and Expropriation

No firm mentioned nationalization or expropriation as factors in determining transfer prices.**
They were cited only as factors in preinvestment decisions. Intracorporate transfers can be used to
minimize subsidiary holdings of liquid assets by
selling to the family everything movable at the lowest possible prices (thereby decreasing stocks), and
to minimize cash holdings by overpaying for real or
fictitious services rendered by the parent. The
probable success of such action is not great, however, because the firms anticipating nationalization or expropriation will probably be under close
surveillance by the government for these and other
reasons.

---

*This was the consensus of the participants in
this study.

**However, they were mentioned by U.S. multi-
national firms in the Business International study.

PARAMETERS FELT TO BE IMPORTANT

Profit centers are not used to a very large extent by non-U.S. multinational companies. As a result, these companies seldom regard transfer pricing as a technique for motivating and evaluating divisional management performance; they view transfer pricing more as a means of control over subsidiary operations. Repeated below are the parameters that U.S. multinational firms think are important for an optimally integrated transfer pricing system.*

1. Providing a fair profit to the producing unit

2. Permitting top management to compare and evaluate the performance of various corporate units

3. Being acceptable to national customs officials for the purpose of duty valuation

4. Being acceptable to national tax authorities and antitrust officials

5. Enabling the purchasing unit to meet profit targets despite the pressure of competitive prices

6. Resulting in a reduction of executive time spent on pricing decisions and mediation of intercorporate pricing disputes

7. Providing control over the pricing practices of foreign subsidiaries to ensure that profit goals will be met

8. Providing management with incentives in both the product divisions and the marketing divisions

_____

*These parameters were cited by the participant firms in the Business International study.

9. Ensuring that there will be a regular and sufficient flow of goods and product information

10. Giving a basis for reflecting actual profits (and costs) to the divisions concerned in order to maintain the control facets of operating against a budget, and preserving the psychological factor of forcing a manager to meet or exceed profit goals with a wider latitude of action than that which is afforded when operating solely against a set budget.

Only five of these parameters were cited by non-U.S. firms as of major importance (numbers 4, 5, 6, 7, and 9); they deal with acceptability, competition, and control.

Acceptability

All companies are significantly concerned about possible conflicts with both host and parent country governments over prices. No company wants a court fight with any government, for in such a conflict the company will lose either way. Should a court decision uphold the government's position, the company will suffer through the imposition of punitive damages, loss of privileges, or a cease and desist order. Even if the company wins (a rare case), it may find that some of its other activities are being investigated, that its property taxes are increased, or that its requests for import permits and foreign exchange are denied or delayed.* Firms also stand to lose because of consumer support for the government via boycotts or brand-switching.**

----

*These government actions are not uncommon in the less-developed countries, although they are rare in the United States.

**In contrast with the foreign subsidiaries of U.S. companies, U.S. subsidiaries of non-U.S. multinational firms favor a low visibility profile and try to minimize public identification with their parents. Since public conflicts with the government

Firms also want to maintain good government relations because of long-range considerations, which most participant firms acknowledged. Since they want to make successful long-term investments in the host countries, they need favorable government attitudes.

Competition

Ensuring that profit goals are met despite competitive price pressures is a normal aim for most firms. To accomplish this, a commonly used method is to undervalue intracompany transfers. A different method may be used when there is also competition in the transferred good's market. Year-end reconciliations between parents and subsidiaries take place when equivalent market prices for the transferred good or service prevent direct transfer price manipulation with the shipment. Yearly adjustments are made by manipulating the charge for an item whose price is less standardized, such as management services. The importance of this "profit under competition" parameter is consistent with the importance given to general levels and types of competition as a variable.

Control

Transfer pricing is regarded by most non-U.S. firms as a control device: control over pricing practices, profits, and flows of goods, services, and information. The parents maintain virtually absolute control over intracompany pricing because this is the most common way in which they can control global financial operations and their results--an essential matter. Preoccupation with control is particularly evident in German and English multinational firms.

Because control rests with the parents, it reduces the executive time that needs to be spent on

would increase the visibility of the link, they are regarded as undesirable.

pricing decisions and mediating intracorporate disputes. If few people have to be consulted and the
power division is one-sided (although admittedly
at some price),* less time needs to be spent on
decision-making.

Performance Evaluation

Several firms mentioned that changes may be
made in their transfer pricing systems. Word has
filtered down that profit centers may be adopted
and that the present transfer pricing system may be
altered so that it won't distort profit center evaluation. Since all of these firms have cost-oriented
systems, the understanding is that their transfer
pricing systems will become market oriented.

SYSTEM ORIENTATION

There was no overwhelmingly dominant pattern
evident from the sample, as only 30 first classified their system's orientation. Seventeen firms
reported an arm's-length (market price) method,
three claimed a market-price-less-commission system,
four mentioned a cost-plus arrangement, and six
called theirs a combination system.** There is
probably a tendency for the firms that responded to
claim the use of a market orientation (because it
is most widely desired by governments), and a tendency for those firms that use cost orientations not
to reply. The accounting firms generally felt that
no single orientation was dominant, but that the
division was approximately 50 percent market-price

---

*Some of the disadvantages include the sub-
sidiary managers' dissatisfaction, the possible
loss of constructive comments and insights, and the
managers' lack of motivation because of their lack
of participation.

**One firm said that it receives management
services at no charge.

oriented, 30 percent cost oriented, and 20 percent
a combination. If their analysis is correct, then
the non-U.S. systems of international transfer pricing are distinctly more market oriented than the
U.S. systems.*

Several distinct patterns of orientation are
evident, even though there is no one preference.
The size of the firm, the nature of the product,
and the nationality of the parent all affect the
choice of system orientation.

Size of the Firm

There is a substantial correlation between the
firm's size and the transfer pricing system orientation: the larger the parent firm, the more likely
it is to use a cost-oriented system. The reasons
advanced by the participants for this are the firm's
ability to differentiate its products, to supply
highly complex cost formulas, and to have a significant influence on the market price.

If a firm can differentiate its product to
such an extent that there is no close market equivalent (and hence no market established price), then
the firm's own cost figures become the most identifiable measure of value for the good being transferred. Product differentiation is not necessarily
restricted to large companies, but they tend to
have more.

The cost systems of larger companies tend to
be more complex than those of smaller companies.
The existence of joint costs and more indirect cost
allocations gives them more discretion in cost-
determination procedures. Edith Penrose's argument
that all costs are arbitrary is well taken, but a

---

*Both the Business International and Confer-
ence Board Record studies reported a predominance
of cost-oriented systems in U.S. multinational
businesses.

larger firm can be more arbitrary. Furthermore,
the greater sophistication of large corporations'
accountants relative to government agency accountants is another factor influencing the choice of a
cost orientation. By presenting a highly complex
and confusing cost formula, the corporation account-
ant can dazzle the government agent, leaving him
little alternative but to accept the company's determination of value.

Differences Related to Products

Market-price-based transfer pricing systems
are common among firms whose products compete in
highly competitive markets. The existence of a
recognized market price (or price range) is the
major determinant, not the position of the buyer in
the economic distribution scheme or the classification of the good being transferred. It cannot be
said that firms that transfer final products use
market prices and those that transfer raw materials
or intermediate goods use cost-oriented prices. Of
the twenty firms reporting the use of a market-
oriented system, eight produce final goods, six
handle intermediate goods, and six manufacture industrial equipment. Of the three firms reporting
straight-cost systems, one produces final goods,
one deals with intermediate goods, and the other
manufactures industrial goods. The six firms using
a combination system are also equally divided among
these categories. This system allows for a differing degree of competition for their various products:
those without much competition are transferred at
cost, while those in more competitive markets are
transferred at market prices.*

------

*An example of a combination system is one
utilized by a European-owned company that manufactures pharmaceutical drugs and chemicals. Basic
chemicals such as hydrochloric acid are transferred
at market prices, while patented medicines are
transferred at cost.

In choosing the market-based system, the de-
cisive factor appears to be the ease with which an
equivalent arm's-length price can be found by a
government agency, although the reliability of the
market price is also important. The problem of reliability can be illustrated by world oil prices.
For years the international oil companies have
claimed operating losses because competition forces
them to sell oil below the established, posted world
prices. They have argued for the use of discounted
prices as the basis for taxable income determination
rather than the posted prices. They feel that the
discounted market prices represent the real market
prices, and that the posted prices are no longer
reliable as a true measure of value. The problem
arises because host governments compute taxes on
what the profits would be if the companies used the
posted prices; this results in higher tax liabilities for the companies in producing countries. The
host governments justify this practice by saying
that the discounted prices are fictitious because
the discounted-price sales are made to "downstream"
subsidiaries of the same company and not on an open
market.

NATIONAL DIFFERENCES

Several distinct cultural patterns are discernible when there is some degree of freedom in choosing the orientation of a transfer pricing system.
This freedom arises largely from the lack of reliable, equivalent market prices for the goods being
transferred, as discussed earlier. In this situation, a firm can transfer either at cost or at market, or somewhere in between. One hypothesis of
this study was that there would be national preferences for specific orientations due to different
culturally based business goals, objectives, and
expectations. These differences do exist and will
be discussed below; although they are highly gener-
alized and do not apply to all firms in a given
country, these differences represent a caricature
of several nations' preferences and systems.

France

The overriding goal of French management is to minimize their income tax. It is no secret that in France, neither individuals nor corporations are fond of paying income taxes; they want to pay as little as possible. This general attitude does not distinguish the French from other national groups, but perhaps their fervor does.[3] It is not surprising, therefore, to find that the French consider the income tax variable as the most important factor in determining transfer prices and that they use their transfer pricing systems to minimize world tax payments.

Low transfer prices (cost-oriented) are used by those firms whose export profits are either tax free or taxed at lower rates. Firms that receive a tax credit on the franc value of their exports (or the amount of foreign currency earned) use high transfer prices. Those firms whose exports are not subject to subsidization or involved in a tax credit arrangement use transfer prices to maximize profit in countries that have the lowest income tax rates.

Several of the accounting partners mentioned that French authorities do not closely examine transfer prices between French corporations and their subsidiaries. This de facto neglect creates additional opportunities and incentives to manipulate transfer prices and optimally arrange corporate taxable income.

None of the respondent French firms use arm's-length prices, but the response rate was too low for this finding to support the pattern described above. One firm uses market-price-less-commission, and two firms use cost-plus prices. Their choice of orientation permits a substantial amount of transfer price manipulation. Profits can be moved around by changing the amount of commission, the cost allocation procedures, or the amount of profit taken by the selling unit (that is, the "plus" in cost-plus).

Italy

Tax minimization also emerges as the major consideration of Italian multinational firms. Unlike the French, Italian companies want to maximize the parent company profits rather than the profits of subsidiaries in countries with low tax rates. The difference in their procedures is largely attributable to income tax determination and collection procedures in Italy. Companies feel that collection procedures are so confused and variously interpreted in Italy that there are maximum opportunities for avoiding or deferring taxes there. If this is true, then market prices will probably be used for intracompany transfers from parents to subsidiaries because they place the transaction's profit in the selling unit (the Italian parent). Conversely, transfers priced at cost can be expected for goods purchased by the parent from its subsidiaries. This pattern was confirmed by several accounting partners, one Italian firm, and several non-Italian firms.*

A comptroller of an Italian-owned subsidiary initially said that competition was the major reason for using market prices. He pointed out that the competitive pricing of the "American giants" of the industry in both input and output markets left no other alternative. However, after further questioning, it became clear that market prices were also used to minimize taxes. The U.S. operation was being evaluated not for its own profits but for its contribution to the parent's profits. By purchasing at arm's-length prices, the subsidiary made such a contribution by allowing all the transaction's profit to accrue to the parent.

----

*Since confirmation of the Italian pattern by non-Italian firms took the form of "Pedro stories," it may be questionable. Several firms mentioned similar stories though, and their impressions of the Italian tax system were consistently negative.

The notoriety of the Italian tax system is
well known, if not well documented. All of the international accounting firm partners agree about
this, since most of them have client problems in
Italy. Their insistence on using U.S. standard accounting principles in Italy is a drawback to their
volume of business, for Italian firms prefer the
more flexible Italian standards and practices that
give them greater opportunities for minimizing
their taxes.

Japan

The Japanese prefer cost-oriented systems,
primarily for price-competitive reasons. No statistical support can be given for this preference
because none of the Japanese firms participated in
this study. The international accountants were
aware of this pattern, however, and the "dumping"
suits brought by the United States against the
Japanese would seem to bear it out.

The intense price-competitiveness of the Japanese in world markets can be attributed in part to
low transfer pricing. Sometimes dumping violations
can be avoided by under-invoicing the manufacturing
inputs to subsidiaries. This procedure allows the
final product to be made and sold at a price close
to what would have been considered dumping if the
final product itself had been exported directly to
the country.* Perhaps because of such under-
invoicing, the Japanese subsidiaries in the United
States did not choose to participate in this study.

England

The major consideration of English firms is
return on investment. Yearly target rates are set
for subsidiary operations, and transfer price manipulation is used to ensure that they will be attained.

---

*Two of the international accounting firms'
partners report such procedures.

Even those companies that use market prices for intracorporate transfers of goods make year-end profit adjustments, customarily in the form of payments for services. English parents often pay inflated prices for technological information supplied by their subsidiaries when the subsidiaries' returns on investments would otherwise be lower than acceptable. A parent's favorable capacity variance may similarly result in a year-end cost reduction adjustment for the goods already purchased by its subsidiaries. On the other hand, the parent will often make adjustments in its favor if the subsidiary's return on investment is too high. One electrical machinery manufacturer moves income among the "surplus" and "deficit" subsidiaries until each attains its target return on investment.

Only three English-owned subsidiaries report the use of straight market prices for intracorporate transfers--the least flexible orientation. Eight others report the use of either cost, market-price-less-commission, or combination systems (the more flexible types). Two of the firms using a combination system transfer goods at market prices but services at cost.

Subsidiary managers feel that the major reason for emphasizing return on investment is a peculiarity of the English banking system. It is their opinion that English bankers demand a steady and predictable return on investment before a loan will be approved. The English parent thus promises an acceptable rate of return for its subsidiary in order to obtain funds to initiate or refinance its operation. The parent company's executives watch the subsidiary rate of return closely because they know that the English bank loan officer will be doing so, too.

Canada

The transfer pricing systems of Canadian firms are distinctly market oriented. Canadian-U.S. trade is subject to both Canadian and U.S. tax

regulations that specify arm's-length prices, making
it doubly difficult to use any other prices. Of the
eight firms that classified their system, only one
does not use market prices. This particular company's U.S. subsidiary is twice the size of its
Canadian parent, and the transfer pricing decisions
are made by the American subsidiary's comptroller.
The products sold are highly differentiated, which
makes a cost-oriented system more feasible.

The long history of good economic and political relations between the United States and Canada
is cited as another factor influencing the choice
of system orientation. Market prices elicit the
least hostility and are generally thought to be the
most equitable. Host countries generally regard
cost orientations as more devious types and most
likely to harm local competition. Market prices
are thus a sound choice for Canada because of the
amount of trade between the two countries and their
geographical proximity.

An interesting example of the one-way trade
pattern mentioned earlier in this chapter is provided by a Canadian paper products company. Wood
pulp, the major input of the subsidiary, is transferred from the Canadian parent via pipeline over a
distance of one and a half miles. Nothing is ever
sent back to the parent through the pipeline nor
shipped in any other way. There have been no argu-
ments over the value of the pulp transferred (because market prices are used), but there have been
disputes between Canadian and U.S. tax officials
over the ownership of the pulp in the pipeline.
The company would often change the ownership of the
pipeline (rather than transfer prices) to its tax
advantage. The issue has now been resolved: the
parent owns the pipeline and its contents.

Germany

The Germans are among the least concerned with
transfer pricing, yet they exercise the closest
control over subsidiary operations of any non-U.S.

group.* Since transfer pricing is the one area over
which even highly decentralized companies exercise
considerable control, the German lack of concern is
surprising. The reason given most often for this
attitude is the German emphasis on the fixed asset
position of operations and long-run stability. German management is not too preoccupied with such criteria as return on investment or yearly profitability, and the managers are not evaluated or rewarded
for these things. Rather, their performance is
evaluated for prudent plant expansion and overall
production efficiency.

Several of the accounting partners cited unfavorable past experiences with inflation and war
as the major reasons for the German emphasis. The
fact that fixed assets increased in value during
and after such periods apparently influences their
present-day thinking. The German corporate financial reports also emphasize the balance sheet rather
than the income statement, and fixed assets precede
current assets on the balance sheet.** Clearly,
transfer pricing is less important and receives
less attention when short-run profitability and return on investment are not major considerations.

Consistent with this cultural attitude, there
seems to be no clear pattern of orientation for
German multinational firms. Two firms report the
use of market prices, one reports the use of cost,
one uses a combination system, and two others do
not know what orientation their parents use. The
accounting partners also could not identify any
dominant pattern.

---

*These two facts were cited by both subsidiary
managers and accounting firm partners.

**The financial reports of U.S. corporations
emphasize the income statement and place current
assets before fixed assets on the balance sheet.

One characteristic pattern that emerges is the
closeness of control retained by German parents
over their subsidiary operations, both in the short
run and in the long run. Two of the firms interviewed are not free to buy from other than their
parent company. Their managers feel that this re-
strictive arrangement is more the rule than the exception for German companies. Their German parents
retain substantial control over final pricing policies, subsidiary operation financing, make-or-buy
decisions, and marketing strategies; they have absolute control of plant expansion and long-run capital commitments. In short, the managers of German-
owned subsidiaries are extremely restricted in the
number of decisions they can make alone; although
they do not like this situation at all, the most
unhappy persons are the American-born officers of
these subsidiaries.

Scandinavia

Scandinavian multinational corporations place
their major emphasis on a single parameter--accept-
ability to host governments. Their transfer prices
are based on the method that will be least likely
to cause trouble with host governments. Consequently, their transactions with U.S. subsidiaries
are made at arm's-length prices, the method pre-
scribed by Section 482 of the U.S. Internal Revenue
Service Code. Arm's-length prices are also used
for intracompany transfers with non-U.S. subsidiaries, even in the absence of specific laws re-
quiring market prices, because governments generally
believe that these prices are the fairest and the
least manipulative. The president of a U.S. subsidiary of a Swedish equipment manufacturer who was
interviewed for this study remarked:

> It is difficult for host countries'
> firms to obtain government sanctions
> against a multinational company mak-
> ing competitive inroads if all of its
> transfers are made at prices it would
> sell to any nonaffiliated company.

> Where market prices exist, they are
> used, and considerable effort is made
> to approximate a fair market price if
> one does not already exist. This is
> the normal Scandinavian pattern.

Host country acceptability is important to
Scandinavian firms because of their worldwide subsidiary operations. Scandinavian markets are small
in relation to other world markets, so the foreign
subsidiary operations of Scandinavian firms are
large in relation to their domestic operations.
Consequently, a major portion of their corporate
family profits comes from subsidiary operations.
Since long-run corporate success is largely contingent upon the long-run success of their foreign operations, Scandinavian managers seek good relationships with host governments.

Acceptability to host countries also helps to
explain the high degree of autonomy that character-
izes Scandinavian-owned subsidiaries. It is felt
that local managers are in the best position to
evaluate both public and government sentiment and
their implications for future corporate operations.
The local managers have the authority to make decisions pertaining to these evaluations. Also, Scandinavian firms recognize that governments prefer
more autonomous subsidiaries because they are less
likely to be influenced by factors operating outside the country (over which the host government
has little or no control).

Australia, Belgium, the Netherlands, and Switzerland

No discernible patterns or attitudes could be
identified for multinational firms of these countries. None of the Australian or Swiss firms participated, and none of the letters received from
the few respondent Belgian and Dutch firms ventured
any generalizations. The international accounting
firm partners also could not generalize about the
transfer pricing systems of these national groups.

TRENDS

Non-U.S. systems of international transfer pricing are moving toward the greater use of market prices and less price manipulation, and transfer prices are becoming more important to firms. These trends were mentioned in both the correspondence and interviews with corporate executives and accounting firm partners. The first two trends are closely related: market prices do not permit as much manipulation as cost-based prices. They will be discussed separately, however, for they have different causes. Transfer pricing has become more important to firms because of increased surveillance by outside groups, the growing volume of transfers due to economic expansion, and the greater integration of international production operations.

Use of Market Prices

Cost-based systems are either being phased out or altered in such a way that they are approaching market-oriented systems.* The major reason for the trend toward using market prices is the growing adoption of tax regulations similar to the U.S. Section 482. Other reasons include a shift toward the greater use of profit centers and return on investment for evaluating subsidiary performance.

In terms of profit centers, it is assumed that each unit is independent of all others and acts accordingly--both buying and selling at market prices. The use of any other prices would be inconsistent with this assumption. Profit center evaluation is much less meaningful if the profit earned by each unit is a function of arbitrary profit allocation.**

---

*One example of this alteration is the addition of a profit margin for the selling unit to the cost so that the cost-plus -profit price is equivalent to the market price.

**Arbitrary profit allocation refers to the decision of how much profit (if any) will be added to the cost price of the transferred good before sale.

Return on investment analysis is also less
meaningful when prices other than market prices
are used. The true value of both the investment
and the return can be substantially altered by
changing the price of goods and services sold internally. Straight-cost transfers lower the real
value of investment goods while increasing the
profit (and hence the returns) on all other goods.
For return on investment figures to be of value,
real cost and sales figures must be used.

Price Manipulation

The use of market prices for intracompany
transfers does not eliminate the possibilities
for manipulation; it only lessens the potential
magnitude. When the volume of a company's output
affects world market prices, transfer prices can
still be manipulated. The use of market-price-
less-commission also permits profit allocation,
since the size of the commission discount will
determine how much of the profit will accrue to
the buyer. The existence of real market equivalents only provides a benchmark for price comparisons, making substantial price manipulation more
readily noticeable. As more companies use market
prices, equivalents will increase in number.

The market price also provides the best measure of product value. Even though the intracompany transaction does not take place within a
real market, the best measure of its worth is
still an arm's-length price: the price at which a
nonaffiliated buyer and seller would arrive. Thus
the shift toward the use of market prices not
only lessens the ability to manipulate prices
but also provides a more meaningful measure of
value.

When cost is the basis, comparisons become
more difficult. Product costs are seldom available or easily obtained. The same product made
in two separate firms may appear to have different costs because of different accounting procedures, even though neither firm can produce the

good more cheaply than the other.* The arbitrary
exclusion or inclusion of certain cost allocations
is another source of apparent cost differences, and
it permits considerable cost (and hence transfer
price) manipulation.

Long-run considerations also influence the degree of price manipulation. Many firms are taking
the Scandinavian position that long-run success is
contingent upon the acceptability of its operating
procedures by both parent and host country governments. Since these governments are taking a closer
look at multinational companies, the use of non-
manipulated transfer prices will arouse less sus-
picion and distrust.

Importance to the Firm

The growing concern about transfer prices
shown by outside groups has increased their importance to the firm. Companies must exercise great
care in order to minimize any negative (unfavorable)
repercussions. The volume of intracompany transfers is also important, for the greater the volume,
the greater the possible distortion of profits. A
company with substantial intracorporate transfers
is more likely to be investigated than one with
smaller amounts.

The volume of internal transfers, however, is
largely a function of the degree of integration of
international operations. Several of the international accounting firm partners said that intracorporate transfers were becoming more important for
this reason. For example, a Canadian firm special-
izing in transportation equipment combines French-
made transmissions, English-made engines, Mexican-
made axles, and U.S.-made sheet metal parts in
order to produce a tractor in Detroit for sale in

------

*One firm may use direct costing while the
other one uses absorption costing, for example.

Canada. Their pattern of international specialization and subsequent product integration is by no means unique. Transfer pricing will inevitably become more important as such production and logistic patterns develop.

Intracompany transfers may also increase because of business prosperity and expansion. The rapid growth of several U.S. subsidiaries has been due to substantial increases in imports from both their non-U.S. parents and their sister subsidiaries. Such growth is also taking place among the parents' subsidiaries in the European Economic Community.

SUMMARY

As a group, U.S. subsidiaries of non-U.S. firms are singularly independent. They are free to operate largely on their own with a minimum of advice and control from their parents. There are national differences in the degree of their autonomy, however. German and English firms maintain the closest control, while Italian and Scandinavian parents maintain the least. The major reason for this independence is the nature of the U.S. market, although the culturally tied philosophy of management is also important.

The non-U.S. parents retain absolute control over transfer pricing, regardless of the degree of subsidiary autonomy that otherwise exists. The prices are set at the home office by the top financial executives, with little (if any) participation by subsidiary managements. One reason for this is that goods and services flow one way from the parents to their subsidiaries. More important, however, is the fact that parent company executives are uniformly unwilling to relinquish control over transfer pricing because it can significantly affect the financial outcome of global operations. The executives have a vested interest in this outcome.

Different methods of transfer pricing are employed to achieve different results. Parents use cost-based transfer prices to keep subsidiaries competitive, to take advantage of various types of export-profit credits, to maximize income in countries with low tax rates, and to lessen ad valorem customs duties. They use market-oriented systems to maximize parent company earnings, to protect against inflation, and to minimize conflicts with governments and other external parties. Year-end adjustments are made in many cases to ensure that profit goals or return on investment targets will be met.

Cultural preferences are reflected in transfer pricing systems when some degree of freedom is permitted in choosing a system. Scandinavian, Canadian, and Italian firms predominantly use market-oriented systems. French, English, and Japanese firms largely use cost-oriented or combination systems. National preferences are attributable to different managerial objectives and attitudes.

A firm's opportunity to choose a particular system depends upon the nature of the competition in both final selling markets and transferred good markets, as well as different legal restrictions. The actual system selected is a function of these legal constraints, the nature of competition in the various markets, and the particular objectives and expectations of management.

The present trend is toward the greater use of market prices and less price manipulation; transfer prices are also becoming more important to firms. These developments are taking place because of pressure from outside groups, and they will continue as subsidiary operations (and intracorporate transfers) increase in value.

NOTES

1.   Jean-Luc Rocour, "Management of European Subsidiaries in the United States," Management International, VI, 1 (1966), 13-27.

2.   Ibid., p. 14. His measures of control were the amount of control exercised by the parent in general policies and functional operations, the amount of information exchanged, and the amount of useful advice provided by the parent.

3.   See Robert Ball, "The Declining Art of Concealing the Figures," Fortune, LXXVI, 4 (September 1967).

**COMPARISONS
AND
CONCLUSIONS**

Internal transfers of goods and services are typical of multinational firms. It is the integration of world operations that gives them their strength, and non-U.S. multinational firms do not differ from their U.S. counterparts in this respect. They often differ in how they view international transfer pricing problems, however. The first part of this chapter presents a summary of the similarities and differences between U.S. and non-U.S. views and intracorporate pricing systems. The second part presents the major conclusions of' this study, some of their broader implications for international business, and related areas that need further research.

COMPARISONS WITH U.S. MULTINATIONAL FIRMS

Organizational Structure

It is difficult to say whether U.S. or non-U.S. multinational firms are more centralized. The largest firms on both sides appear to be similarly organized. Operationally, however, non-U.S. multinational firms seem to be more fragmented.[1] Their subsidiaries assume a lower visibility profile and make more efforts at accommodation than innovation.[2]

U.S. subsidiaries, however, are the least controlled of any group of subsidiaries. G. P. Lauter, in his article "Sociological-Cultural and Legal Factors Impeding Decentralization of Authority in Developing Countries," concluded that a negative view of authority in the host country is the most important impediment to decentralization.[3] If the converse of this hypothesis were true, then firms operating in countries where there is a favorable view of authority would be more decentralized. This could account for the fact that U.S. national companies and U.S. subsidiaries of non-U.S. multinational companies have a high degree of autonomy. It could also account for the fact that there is a higher degree of control exercised by all multinational firms over subsidiary operations in developing countries.

Other plausible explanations include the relatively higher sophistication of the U.S. market, the relatively larger size of U.S. subsidiaries, the relatively higher degree of competition and change in the United States, and the relatively tougher legal restrictions in the United States. These explanations were suggested by the firms in this study as well as those investigated by Jean-Luc Rocour.

It is less easy to account for national differences in the degree of decentralization. The relatively larger size of Italian- and Scandinavian-owned subsidiaries vis-à-vis their parents is a possible explanation. Several studies have portrayed German and British managers as being more conservative than their European counterparts and have pointed out other differences as well.[4] The participants in this study also had consistent stereotypes of national management groups.

Locus of Transfer Price Decision-Making

Transfer prices are set by the parent company financial executives for both U.S. and non-U.S. firms. The size of the participating staff varies

but cannot be correlated with any specific corporate
characteristic. In no case does the person responsible for setting prices have a rank lower than
treasurer, and in most cases he is the financial
vice-president or comptroller. Disputes are settled
by parent company executives--usually by the president and all of the vice-presidents. This same
group sets the broad guidelines for transfer prices
and approves all major changes in orientation or
policy.

Subsidiary participation is almost nonexistent.
Subsidiary managers have virtually no voice in
transfer price determination; often they are not
even free to reject the price or to buy elsewhere.
Their greatest opportunity to participate is when
intracorporate transfers are infrequent but high in
value, or when their operations are larger than the
parent's.

Sophistication of the Transfer
Pricing System

Non-U.S. systems are generally less sophisticated than U.S. systems, except for the largest
non-U.S. multinational firms. In an extremely candid letter from the comptroller of a German chemical company, he cited "expediency" as the basis for
establishing most transfer prices. He also said
that the lack of a scientific approach to the problem was common among non-U.S. firms.

Sophistication is associated also with system
orientation. Market-oriented systems are less
sophisticated because they do not rely on complex
cost determination formulas. Since market-oriented
systems are quite common among non-U.S. multinational firms, this may also account for their lower
degree of system sophistication.

Variables Considered

All multinational companies seem to take the
same variables into account when they formulate

their guidelines for transfer prices. The major
variables considered only by non-U.S. firms are export subsidies and tax credits; these are important
primarily for French, English, and Italian firms.
A straight comparison of the relative importance of
the different variables to U.S. and non-U.S. firms
cannot be made because of national variances among
the non-U.S. firms. Country-by-country comparisons
can be made, however, and these are summarized in
Table 4. National differences in the importance
placed on these variables are a function of the different objectives and philosophies of management,
which was discussed in Chapter 4.

Parameters Considered

Non-U.S. multinational firms do not take into
account as many parameters as their U.S. counterparts. As mentioned in Chapter 4, non-U.S. firms
consider only about half of the ten parameters
cited by U.S. firms.* The parameters that are generally ignored pertain to transfer pricing's relation to management performance evaluation. Since
non-U.S. companies do not often use profit centers
and return on investment analysis, they do not regard problems caused by transfer pricing in these
areas as important. The English, however, do rate
these considerations as important.

National differences account for different
managerial philosophies. The U.S. emphasis on
yearly profits and return on investment contrasts
sharply with the Scandinavian emphasis on acceptability to host governments and long-run profitability. The German emphasis on fixed assets, cost
efficiency, and prudent plant expansion differs
substantially from the French desire to minimize
world tax payments. Table 5 presents a summary of
these and other national differences.

---

*See pages 75-76.

TABLE 4

National Differences in Relative Importance Given to Variables in Transfer Price Determination

Variables	Parent Nationality						
	U.S.	Canada	France	Germany	Italy	Scandinavia	England
Income tax	1	1	1	3	1	3	3
Customs duties	2	2	2	3	3	3	3
Inflation	1	2	2	2	2	3	2
Changes in currency exchange rates	3	3	2	2	3	3	2
Exchange controls	2	3	5	5	5	5	5
Improving financial appearance of subsidiary	3	3	3	4	4	4	1
Expropriation	3	3	5	5	5	5	5
Export subsidies and tax credits	4	2	2	4	2	4	2
Level of competition	4	2	2	3	2	3	3

Weighting Scale:

1 = high importance
2 = medium importance
3 = low importance
4 = not mentioned
5 = mentioned only with respect to non-U.S. operations

Source: Correspondence and interviews with subsidiary executives and international accounting firm partners.

TABLE 5

National Differences in Relative Importance Given to Parameters in Transfer Price Determination

Parameters	U.S.*	Non-U.S.	Parent Nationality					
			Canada	France	Germany	Italy	Scandinavia	England
Provide a fair profit to the producing unit	1	2	2	2	2	2	2	2
Permit top management to compare and evaluate the performance of various corporate units	1	2	2	2	2	2	2	2
Be acceptable to national customs officials for the purpose of duty valuation	1	1	1	2	1	2	1	1
Be acceptable to national tax authorities and antitrust officials	1	1	1	2	1	2	1	1
Enable the purchasing unit to meet profit targets despite the pressure of competitive prices	1	1	1	1	2	1	2	1
Result in a reduction of executive time spent on pricing decisions and mediation of intercorporate pricing disputes	1	1	2	1	1	1	2	1
Provide control over the pricing practices of foreign subsidiaries to ensure that profit goals will be met	1	1	1	1	1	1	2	1

| Parameters | U.S.* | Non-U.S. | Parent Nationality | | | | | |
			Canada	France	Germany	Italy	Scandinavia	England
Provide management with incentives in both the product divisions and the marketing divisions	1	2	2	2	2	2	2	2
Insure that there will be a regular and sufficient flow of goods and product information	1	2	1	2	2	2	2	2
Give a basis for reflecting actual profits (and costs) to maintain the control facets of operating against a budget, and preserve the psychological factor of forcing a manager to meet or exceed profit goals with a wider latitude of action than that which is afforded when operating solely against a set budget	1	2	2	2	2	2	2	2

Weighting Scale:

1 = important
2 = less important

*No relative weightings are identifiable for U.S. multinational firms.

Source: Correspondence and interviews with subsidiary executives and international accounting firm partners.

System Orientation

Similarities and differences are discernible in terms of company size, competition in the product markets, and national preferences. Generally speaking, however, U.S. systems of international intracorporate pricing are more cost oriented, while non-U.S. systems are more market oriented.

The greatest similarity in systems is found among the large multinational firms. They have highly sophisticated cost-oriented systems regardless of parent nationality. They usually maintain additional records using market-price equivalents for subsequent management performance evaluations and do considerable maneuvering of liquid assets. The smallest multinational firms tend to have market-oriented systems and do considerably less maneuvering of income. Their degree of production integration is smaller, and their volume of intracompany transfers is less. Consequently the smaller firms are less concerned with intracompany pricing.

The largest differences in systems are found among the medium to large size multinational firms whose products or environments permit them some choice of system orientation. The major differentiating factor is the degree of competition in the product markets. Firms that can operate with some monopoly in their product markets use cost-oriented systems, while those that cannot do not. Corporate size differences may account for the small differences in systems adopted by the largest multinational firms. Their size alone gives them monopoly power in the markets where they operate, and thus they tend to view the intracorporate pricing problem in the same perspective. This similarity in perspective may support the hypothesized existence of James Burnham's "third culture," in which the managers of large companies in highly industrialized societies tend to become a distinct class, regardless of the prevailing system.*

*This type of management is required for the operation of what Charles Kindleberger defines as the international corporation. See page 8.

Apart from the largest multinational firms, there are differences in national preferences. The French prefer non-market-oriented systems because they can thus minimize world tax payments. The English also prefer a cost orientation, but their goal is to achieve their target return on investment rates. The Italians use market-oriented systems to maximize corporate income in Italy, which is equivalent to minimizing their tax liability. Canadians also employ market-oriented systems, but essentially because of specific government regulations and a desire to maintain good relations with other governments. The Scandinavian firms view good relations with other governments as paramount, and consequently they are the biggest supporters and users of market-oriented systems. The Germans are the least concerned about transfer pricing, do not seem to prefer any given orientation, and do not exhibit any dominant pattern. However, new German regulations will probably force a shift to more market-oriented systems. Additional similarities and differences in specific areas are presented in Tables 4 and 5.

Trends

Several major trends are evident in all systems of international intracorporate pricing. Market-oriented systems are being used increasingly, and transfer pricing is becoming more important to firms. The growth in the volume of international transfers because of economic expansion and greater integration of global operations adds to the potential profit distortion. The increased potential brings greater surveillance by outside groups, which demand the use of market prices and sometimes specific government regulations. There are also internal pressures to use market prices because of the widespread use of profit centers to evaluate subsidiary performance, a concept that requires the use of market prices.

Companies of all nationalities are experiencing these external and internal pressures, which are growing in significance. These pressures may lead to greater uniformity in system orientation and eliminate many of the national differences.

CONCLUSIONS PERTAINING TO THE HYPOTHESES

Hypotheses formulated for this study were designed to narrow the scope of the research and serve
as a basis for drawing conclusions. It was not anticipated that they would be statistically valid in
all cases or in all respects. The major differentiating factor in terms of their applicability is
the size of the multinational corporation.

Hypothesis One states that all multinational
firms face the same environmental problems with respect to international intracorporate pricing. The
conclusion of this research is that this hypothesis
is correct for the very large multinational firms
but not for others. The problems encountered are
largely a function of the number of different environments in which a company operates, and the
smaller multinational firms do not operate in as
many. Some firms operate only in relatively stable
political and economic environments, while others
do not. Thus, many companies do not encounter problems with exchange controls, devaluation, or expropriation. Since most of the non-U.S. firms do not
employ profit centers or return on investment analysis, they do not perceive transfer pricing as caus-
ing problems in these areas either.

However, multinational firms that operate in
the same countries do face essentially the same environmental problems. Whatever differences exist
are due to product differences, for example, tariffs
imposed on certain products but not on others.

Hypothesis Two states that not all multinational corporations perceive the importance of the
transfer pricing problem in the same way. This hypothesis appears to be correct because there are
differences in this perception even among the large
multinational companies. Perception of the problem
varies according to the diversity of international
operations, the degree of competition, the nature
of the product, and the parent company nationality.
For example, customs duties are not as important a

problem for intracorporate transfers within the
Common Market as they are for German-U.S. trade.
Similarly, value determination and justification
are not perceived as important problems for firms
that use market prices because highly competitive
markets establish recognizable equivalents, while
these problems are important for firms that use
cost-based transfer prices. Profit center performance evaluation and return on investment analysis
are not important for most non-U.S. multinational
firms because they are not widely employed, while
these factors are cited as being quite important
by U.S. multinational firms.

Hypothesis Three states that differences in
importance perception are a function of differing
cultural influences. While cultural differences in
philosophy and objectives are a major cause, they
are not the only one. However, they help explain
differences in importance perception when different
nationality firms operate in the same environment.
A Scandinavian, a German, and an English equipment
manufacturer will each give a different emphasis to
environmental problems and operational parameters
even though they all produce similar equipment in
the United States. The Scandinavian firm will view
acceptability to the host government as the most
important factor; the English firm will view return
on investment as the most important consideration;
the German will not think either of these is important. Tables 4 and 5 show the existence of these
cultural differences.

Hypothesis Four states that cultural differences lead to different international intracorporate
pricing systems. As with the finding of Hypothesis
Three, cultural differences appear to be only one
influence. Other important influences are differences in international operation size and diversity,
degrees of competition, legal restrictions, and
types of products. Various transfer pricing systems used by firms of differing nationality can be
often explained by cultural differences. A Scandinavian firm will use market prices because they

are the most acceptable to host governments; an
English firm will use cost-based prices because
they permit the necessary manipulation often required to ensure that returns on investment targets
will be met; and a German firm will use a combination system because it allows the firm to employ
market prices when they are available and costs
when they are not.

Cultural differences in the philosophy and objectives of management are often modified by other
environmental considerations, however. The big international aluminum and petroleum companies have
similar systems and viewpoints regardless of parent
company nationality. The smaller firms that operate in markets where there are recognized market
prices and legal regulations specifying their use
employ market-oriented intracorporate pricing systems.

Hypothesis Five states that no single transfer
pricing system is optimal for all multinational
corporations. The findings of this study suggest
that this hypothesis is correct. The different
philosophies, objectives, environments, products,
degrees of production integration, and sizes of
multinational firms preclude the possibility that
any transfer pricing system would be universally
optimal. A corollary is that there is no single
quantifiable solution procedure that would be uniformly applicable for deriving optimal international intracorporate prices. An optimal system
could possibly be developed for the truly international corporation envisioned by Kindleberger,* in
which business philosophies, objectives, and operations are supranational, but at present this type
of international corporation does not exist.

---

*See page 8.

SECOND-ORDER CONCLUSIONS

Other major conclusions of this study are as follows:

1.   International intracorporate pricing is one of the most closely controlled corporate operations, regardless of parent nationality.

2.   The high degree of control over transfer pricing is invariant with respect to the company's degree of central authority over other areas of corporate decision-making.

3.   The degree of participation and influence by subsidiaries is minimal, despite their power and independence in other areas. This is true even for the most autonomous subsidiary group--the U.S. subsidiaries of non-U.S. multinational corporations.

4.   Transfer pricing policy is determined by parent company executives and executed by the top ranking financial officer.

5.   U.S. systems of international intracorporate pricing are distinctly more cost oriented and more complex than non-U.S. systems.

6.   The very large multinational companies of all nationalities exhibit the smallest differences in system orientation and views of attendant problems. They take into account essentially the same variables and parameters, and they utilize similar techniques.

7.   There are pervasive and increasing pressures for uniformity. These pressures are coming from both external and internal sources, and they are responsible for the trend toward the greater use of market-oriented systems and for the increasing importance given to transfer pricing by corporate management.

IMPLICATIONS

The major implication of this study pertains
to the finding of Hypothesis Five--that there is no
universally optimal system of international intracorporate pricing. One has only to think of the
problems of a single multinational firm--the buying,
producing, and selling of hundreds of different raw
materials, semifinished goods, and finished goods
in several constantly changing economic, social,
and political environments--to appreciate the magnitude of the problem of intracorporate pricing.*
It is unlikely that any single transfer pricing system could always be optimal for even one firm under
these circumstances and with diverse management objectives. When there are additional firms with differing objectives, products, and environments, the
possibility of reaching a uniform solution appears
impossible; in fact, it is impossible with existing
quantitative and qualitative models.

It may well turn out that the "optimal" system
is one that minimizes conflicts with external
groups, such as governments. If so, then multinational firms have much to learn from the Scandinavian companies whose systems are designed to meet
this criterion. Since there is an increasing concern being shown by external groups over transfer
pricing, this development may mean trouble for
those firms whose systems are not market oriented
and hence show considerable profit distortion.

A second implication pertains to the effect of
using prices other than market prices for corporate
financial reports and international trade statistics. The potential distortion of reported corporate income becomes greater as the volume of intracompany transfers increases. This is true for any
multinational company, but applies especially in
the case of non-U.S. companies, whose methods and

---

*See Appendixes A and B for further elabora-
tion of this point.

degrees of disclosure confuse even the experts.[5]
Investing in corporations that do not report the
volume and value of intracorporate transfers, which
affect their reported financial position, can be
very hazardous. The use of prices other than market prices for intracorporate transfers can similarly distort international trade figures. The
value of a country's imports from another country
may be understated if the exporting firms consistently sell at undervalued transfer prices to their
importing subsidiaries. If all multinational firms
used market prices for all of their intracorporate
transactions, undoubtedly there would be changes in
the balance of trade. The use of "swap" arrangements such as those in the aluminum and petroleum
industries may also be distorting balance-of-trade
statistics. Creation of the accounts receivable
and payable between the two nonaffiliated parent
companies shows up as short-term direct investments
rather than as entries in the trade sector (the
current account).

A third implication pertains to the different
emphasis placed on transfer pricing by corporate
executives and academicians. Executives view transfer pricing as an extremely important area of
decision-making, and many of them regard it as the
most critical short-run decision. The fact that
only top ranking executives participate in determining these prices indicates their importance.
Academicians, on the other hand, do not accord such
high importance to transfer pricing either domestically or internationally. The subject is treated
only very superficially in business-school texts or
collections of readings, and most of these books
discuss intracorporate pricing as if it were a
peculiar accounting problem for domestic operations.
Thus, most graduate business students know little
or nothing about one of the most important ongoing
financial decision areas of a firm. This inadequate
treatment of transfer pricing by academicians may be
in large part responsible for the lack of scientific
approaches to the problem.

The fourth implication pertains to the bene-
fits of cross-cultural research. There is much to
be learned from studying how other cultures view a
given problem and how they go about solving it.
Such research not only forces one to clarify and
reexamine his own conceptions and solutions but may
point to better alternatives. This study has shown
that non-U.S. corporations do view international
transfer pricing problems differently, and that
they have developed their own methods to solve or
circumvent them. Some of their views and solutions
are better (in some sense) than U.S. ones, and some
are not as good, but they do present viable alternatives. This study has shown that the problems ex-
perienced by U.S. multinational firms are not unique.
The fact that there is tremendous diversity in transfer pricing systems shows that there is neither national nor international agreement on what consti-
tutes the optimal system. Perhaps an interchange
of views and information on the relative successes
of similar systems under different circumstances
and different systems under similar circumstances
would provide useful answers to the problem.

A fifth implication is that corporate size may
exert a harmonizing influence on different philosophies of national management. Since the larger multinational firms can take better advantage of unified global operations, they exhibit closer control
and more centralization than smaller multinational
firms. On the whole they perceive the same basic
problems of operation because they (or their executives) have encountered similar ones. If national
differences in views and systems decrease as corporate size increases, then perhaps the behavior
of large corporations will become more predictable.
The substantial differences in intranational management philosophies discovered by Mason Haire,
Edwin Ghiselli, and Lyman Porter may have been due
to a corporate size factor;* that is, the differences in management philosophy within a nation may

_____

*They report greater differences among managers
within a given country than among managers in different countries.

be attributable to differences in the size of the
corporations for which the managers work. If so,
then James Burnham's prediction about the emerging
"third culture" may be coming true.*

A final implication is that it is still important for outside groups to increase their knowledge
about international intracorporate pricing. If the
potential income distortion is increasing as it appears to be, then groups that will be affected
should take countervailing measures to lessen the
chance (and size) of such distortion. The new regulations pertaining to transfer prices issued in the
United States, Canada, and Germany, and the joint
action taken by the Middle Eastern oil-producing
countries (O.P.E.C.) are good examples of such measures. Nongovernmental groups should also become
more knowledgeable, although probably government
legislation alone can compel disclosure of intracorporate pricing systems.

AREAS NEEDING FURTHER RESEARCH

This study was an exploratory one as well as a
continuation of past research on international transfer pricing. Several major areas remain either un-
explored or in need of further study. Much needs
to be learned about non-U.S. systems, especially
how successful they have been vis-à-vis each other
and U.S. systems. Such research could focus on the
relative successfulness of different systems in
terms of profit maximization, security of capital,
competitive position maintenance, intracorporate
conflict avoidance, goal congruence, and interper-
sonal behavior. It would also be valuable to dis-
cover the extent to which specific systems have
been successful in minimizing environmental conflicts.

Additional and potentially different information about non-U.S. systems and viewpoints could be
obtained from the non-U.S. parents. Sometimes

*See page 104.

subsidiary managers have different perspectives of
what business operations are designed to achieve
and how they are affected by environmental factors.
These managers are also less qualified to speak
about the firm's global policies and operations.
Conducting on-location research with parent company
executives would require a substantial amount of
money and time, but it might be worth it.

Enlarging the sample and changing the
information-generating technique may offer a way
to secure additional insights that would permit
broader, more valid generalizations and provide a
better base from which to make inferences and pre-
dictions. Further research could include the non-
U.S. multinational companies that do not have U.S.
subsidiaries or that are not in the field of manufacturing. Specific questionnaires could be used
to verify the findings of this particular study.
More executives could also be interviewed, since
this method proved to be highly effective in ob-
taining usable information.

A study of one particular industry might also
be valuable.* A fully integrated industry, such
as petroleum, offers the most complex system and
series of interrelationships. The petroleum industry also appears to do the most transfer price manipulation and maneuvering of income, but of all
industries the least amount of information is pub-
licly known about this one. Focusing on one industry would also offer an opportunity to examine the
extent of cultural differences in transfer pricing
systems and views within a given industry-
environment. In addition, such focusing would
provide an opportunity to check the importance of
corporate size with respect to transfer pricing
philosophies and systems.

An interesting study could be made of patterns
of transfer pricing and dividend policies; it might

----

*James Shulman also mentioned this possibility
as worthwhile.

disclose which of the two major methods of maneuvering liquid assets is the most important and how well they work together to attain corporate objectives.

Finally, additional research is needed to decide if there is a feasible quantitative approach. David Rutenberg's model is admittedly a deterministic solution procedure, but it is at least a step in the right direction. As he points out, stochastic programming with recourse permits flexibility in planning for risk so long as updated information can be <u>inputted</u> at only one instant in time.[6] Rutenberg also alludes to the possible use of the maximum principle of the caconical equations of Pontrygin as extended to stochastic control systems by Harold Kushner and F. C. Shweppe.[7] It would be interesting to see if such quantitative methods could be used to determine optimal transfer prices for international operations, even though it appears doubtful.

SUMMARY

Occasionally there is a tendency to underestimate the importance of exploratory research and to regard only experimental work as "scientific." However, if experimental work is to have either theoretical or social value, it must be relevant to broader issues than those posed in the experiment. Such relevance can result only from adequate exploration of the dimensions of the problem with which the research is attempting to deal. . . . The most careful methods during the later stages of an investigation are of little value if an incorrect or irrelevant start has been made.[8]

The alleged importance of international transfer pricing was well substantiated by the

participants in this study, since it comprises one
of the most crucial areas of both short-run and
long-run corporate decision-making. This study set
out to explore non-U.S. systems of international
intracorporate pricing and to compare them with
those of U.S. multinational corporations, and it
has been successful in achieving these objectives.
Its conclusions explain the differences in the problems perceived and encountered and in the methods
that are used to solve or circumvent them. Much
additional work needs to be done, however, to further verify the conclusions of this study and to
explore related areas.

NOTES

1. John Fayerweather, in his book, _Interna-
tional Business Management_ (New York: McGraw-Hill,
1970), delineates two opposing operational strategies for global operations--unification and frag-
mentation. The fragmented approach is where subsidiaries accommodate to national practices, policies, and customs rather than operate on the basis
of a single, worldwide _modus operandi_ (the unified
approach).

2. Accommodation is a sister strategy to frag-
mentation. See Chapter 4 in _ibid_.

3. Lauter used the Delphi technique to determine which of the constraints set forth by Farmer
and Richman were the most critical. For a list of
the constraints, see Richard Farmer and Barry Richman, _International Business: An Operational Theory_
(Homewood, Ill.: Richard D. Irwin, 1966). Lauter's
article appeared in the _Academy of Management Jour-
nal_, XII, 3 (September 1969), 367-78.

4. See D. G. Clark and T. M. Mosson, "Industrial Managers in Belgium, France, and the U.K.,"
Management International, VII, 2 and 3 (1967),
95-100; David Grannick, _The European Executive_
(London: Wiedenfield and Nicholson, 1962); and

Mason Haire, Edwin Ghiselli, and Lyman Porter, _Managerial Thinking_ (New York: John Wiley, 1966).

5.   See Robert Ball, "The Declining Art of Concealing the Figures," _Fortune_ (September 1967), and "Lifting Corporate Curtains," _Fortune_, LXXIII, 3 (March 1966).

6.   See D. W. Walkup and R. J. B. Wets, "Stochastic Programming with Recourse," _S.I.A.M. Journal of Applied Mathematics_, XV, 5 (September 1967), 1299-314; and David Rutenberg, "Maneuvering Liquid Assets in a Multinational Company: Formulation and Deterministic Solution Procedures," _Management Science_, XVI, 10 (June 1970), 672.

7.   See Harold Kushner and F. C. Shweppe, "A Maximum Principle for Stochastic Control Systems," _Journal of Mathematical Analysis and Applications_, VIII (March 1964), 287-302; and Rutenberg, "Maneuvering Liquid Assets in a Multinational Company," p. 672.

8.   Claire Selltiz _et al._, _Research Methods in Social Relations_ (New York: Holt, Rinehart and Winston, 1962), p. 52.

APPENDIXES

THE COMPLEXITY
OF THE
TRANSFER PRICING
PROBLEM

Consider the problems of a large European multinational firm. The principal activities of the
corporate family consist of the manufacture and
sale of pharmaceutical products, veterinary products and animal-feedstuff concentrates, toiletries,
cosmetics, home remedies, and food and drink products. The company is organized into four major
divisions: the pharmaceutical division, the product division, the European division, and the Western Hemisphere division; the latter handles operations for the United States, Canada, Latin America,
Australia, and New Zealand. The parent operates 62
subsidiaries in all, but only 8 are wholly owned.
Several of the subsidiaries themselves have ownership in other subsidiaries. The parent's subsidiaries are located in 24 different countries and in
all four quadraspheres.* Sales in 1970 totaled
£161 million, more than half of which were made outside the parent's country; of the reported group
profit of £30 million, two-thirds was attributable
to international operations.

Intracorporate transfers comprise nearly one-
half of the group sales, but the transfer prices

---

*See Chart 2.

CHART 2

A European Firm's International
Organizational Chart

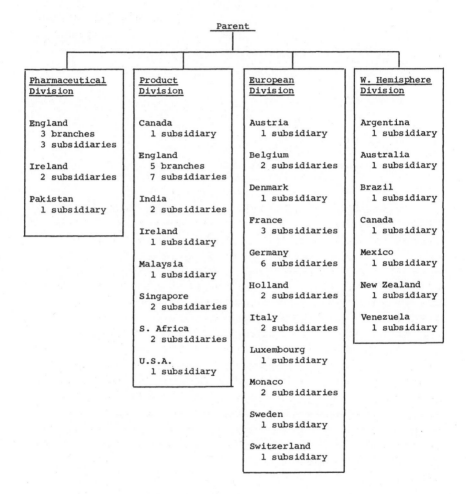

Parent

Pharmaceutical Division	Product Division	European Division	W. Hemisphere Division
England 3 branches 3 subsidiaries Ireland 2 subsidiaries Pakistan 1 subsidiary	Canada 1 subsidiary England 5 branches 7 subsidiaries India 2 subsidiaries Ireland 1 subsidiary Malaysia 1 subsidiary Singapore 2 subsidiaries S. Africa 2 subsidiaries U.S.A. 1 subsidiary	Austria 1 subsidiary Belgium 2 subsidiaries Denmark 1 subsidiary France 3 subsidiaries Germany 6 subsidiaries Holland 2 subsidiaries Italy 2 subsidiaries Luxembourg 1 subsidiary Monaco 2 subsidiaries Sweden 1 subsidiary Switzerland 1 subsidiary	Argentina 1 subsidiary Australia 1 subsidiary Brazil 1 subsidiary Canada 1 subsidiary Mexico 1 subsidiary New Zealand 1 subsidiary Venezuela 1 subsidiary

are not uniformly based. Sales of toiletries, cosmetics, food and drink products, and home remedies
are customarily made at arm's-length prices. The
reason given for this is the availability of market
equivalents, but governmental concern and surveillance are becoming increasingly important. Sales
in these areas account for 62 percent of the total
group sales but only 40 percent of the total group
profit. In these areas there is the least amount
of internal trading.

Cost is the basis for all other intracorporate
sales. The two largest product groups are pharma-
ceuticals and veterinary products and animal-
feedstuff concentrates. They comprise 36 percent
of sales but 50 percent of total group profits.
The cost base is full input cost plus an overhead
recovery allocation. A profit margin is added to
the base cost--usually 15 percent for bulk goods
and 25 percent for finished goods. The markup
varies considerably from time to time and from
country to country, however. The stated goal is to
conform to the legal requirements of host countries,
but where there are none, variations occur in transfer prices. The firm uses a very high landed cost
with a full profit recovery in most developing
countries in order to get the money out of these
areas and protect itself against price controls.
Intracorporate transfers to subsidiaries in more
stable environments are made at much lower prices,
particularly to those countries with lower tax
rates. Any of these prices are subject to change,
however, because return on investment and profit
center performance are of major importance, and
they often require transfer price manipulation and
adjustments.

The point is that the different objectives,
products, environments, and operations of this company do not permit a single transfer price orientation to be optimal at all times or even at a given
point in time. No single system orientation could
be optimal for all firms at all times if it cannot
even be optimal for one firm at a particular time.

B

The size of the international operation and the
number of environments are not always the causes of
system orientation problems. The characteristics of
a single environment can also create difficulties in
selecting an optimal system orientation. Consider
the table below. All of the environmental characteristics on the left side call for the use of market prices, while those on the right call for cost-
based prices, ceteris paribus, given the basic corporate objectives of profit maximization, security
of capital, and competitive position maintenance.
Seldom do the characteristics of a real world environment all line up as nicely as those on the
chart. When characteristics from both sides are
present, selecting an optimal orientation is difficult.

Suppose a country has high income tax rates,
high customs duties, intense price competition in
the company's product market, restrictions on dividend remittances and on the value of goods that can
be imported, high rates of inflation, and a banking
community that makes loans on the basis of a subsidiary's financial position. If market prices are
used for transfers to the subsidiary, then higher
duties will have to be paid, the competitive position of the subsidiary may suffer, fewer goods can
be imported, and the subsidiary will not appear to

be profitable. By using market prices, however, the
parent will succeed in paying lower taxes, getting
the largest amount of liquid funds out, and obtain-
ing the most control over pricing practices. The
use of cost-based transfer prices would produce the
opposite results. Thus either system orientation
would have both favorable and unfavorable results.

If the environmental characteristics remained
the same, then a weighting scale could be devised to
maximize the possible gains or to minimize the possible losses. But these characteristics do change
in importance and in number; if such changes are
material enough, they may dictate a change in system
orientation. Further complications are added when
the firm operates in more than one environment, each
with different characteristics and different rates
of change. All of these differences make it virtually impossible for a single system orientation to
be always optimal: it may work in one environment
for one period of time but cause problems in other
environments at the same time or at a later time.

Conditions in Foreign Country Calling for
Specific Transfer Pricing Policy from the
Domestic Parent to its Foreign Subsidiary

Low Transfer Price

1. Existence of restric-
tions on investment dollar
outflows from the United
States
2. Existence of need to
improve the profit picture
of the subsidiary
3. Existence of intense
price competition
4. Existence of exchange
restrictions on the value
of the amount of goods the
subsidiary can import
5. Existence of a de-
sire to circumvent parts
of the IRS code
6. Existence of a de-
sire to subsidize ineffi-
cient subsidiaries

High Transfer Price

1. Low import duties
2. Higher income tax
3. High rates of
inflation
4. High danger of
devaluation
5. Unstable and un-
friendly government
(danger of expropria-
tion)
6. Existence of ex-
change restrictions on
dividend remittances
or other profit re-
patriations
7. Less than a 50
percent owned sub-
sidiary

JEFFREY ARPAN is Assistant Professor of Accounting and a member of the Institute of International Business at Georgia State University, where he teaches international business, comparative management, and international accounting.

Professor Arpan received his doctorate at Indiana University, where he was an International Business Fellow and Instructor in the International Business Department. While at Indiana, he was awarded membership in Phi Beta Kappa and other honorary societies, and was named James Moffat Scholar in Economics. Professor Arpan's dissertation, upon which this book is based, won the National Dissertation Competition Award of the Association for Education in International Business.

Dr. Arpan's research interests include the study of non-U.S. multinational firms, the effect of culture on multinational firm management, Far Eastern and Eastern European cultures, international accounting, and the social responsibilities of large corporations. He has published articles in the Journal of International Business Studies, the Academy of Management Journal, Business Horizons, and the Atlanta Economic Review.